SPIRITUAL MOTHERING

Spiritual Mothering

The Titus 2 Model for Women Mentoring Women

SUSAN HUNT

CROSSWAY

WHEATON, ILLINOIS

Spiritual Mothering

Copyright © 1992 by Susan Hunt

Published by Crossway
          1300 Crescent Street
          Wheaton, Illinois 60187

First edition published 1992
Second edition published 1993
Reprinted with new cover 2009

Cover design: Amy Bristow
Cover photo: The Bridgeman Art Library

Printed in the United States of America

Throughout the book, names and details of a few women and their stories have been changed to protect their privacy.

Unless otherwise noted, all Scripture quotations are from *The Holy Bible, New International Version*®. © 1973, 1978, 1984 International Bible Society. Used by permission of Zondervan Publishing House. All rights reserved.

The "NIV" and "New International Version" trademarks are registered in the United States Patent and Trademark Office by International Bible Society. Use of either trademark requires the permission of International Bible Society.

All Scripture quotations marked as NASB are from *The New American Standard Bible*®, © 1960, 1962, 1968, 1971, 1973, 1975, 1977, by The Lockman Foundation and are used by permission.

A Leader's Guide for *Spiritual Mothering* is available for small group study. To order, call the Christian Education Publications Bookstore at 1-800-283-1357, or order from your local Christian bookstore.

ISBN: 978-1-4335-0313-9
ISBN PDF: 978-1-4335-1062-5
ISBN Mobipocket: 978-1-4335-1063-2

Crossway is a publishing ministry of Good News Publishers.

VP		19	18	17	16	15	14	13	12	11
14	13	12	11	10	9	8	7	6	5	4

To my granddaughter,
Mary Kate Barriault,
with the prayer that
God will raise up women of faith
who will spiritually mother her generation.

*We will tell the next generation
the praiseworthy deeds of the LORD, his power,
and the wonders he has done . . . so that the next
generation would know them, even the children yet to
be born, and they in turn would tell their children.
Then they would put their trust in God and
would not forget his deeds but
would keep his commands.*
(Psalm 78:4, 6–7)

CONTENTS

ACKNOWLEDGMENTS

Nothing I do is a solo effort. There are many contributors. My husband, Gene, cushions my life with love, balances it with laughter, and surrounds it with prayer.

I am grateful to our children and their spouses for their interest in this part of my life, their encouragement, and their willingness for me to share our experiences.

I thank my mother for many things, but especially for the "stories" of my family heritage. The knowledge that my great-grandmother prayed for the generations to come gives me great joy.

George and Karen Grant and Georgia Settle believed in this project. Without their encouragement and involvement it is doubtful that I would have persevered.

My colleagues at the Christian Education office of the Presbyterian Church in America are wonderful. I especially thank Dennis Bennett, Jane Brooks, Charles and Colleen Dunahoo, John Dunahoo, Debbie Trickett, and Stacey UpDeGraff for their support of this effort.

I am grateful to the senior pastor, Todd Allen, and the elders of my church for providing a context where the gifts and relationships of women flourish.

I am indebted to the women who share their spiritual mothering stories interspersed within this book. These stories are the driving force of the book. I am confident that the reader will share my gratitude to these women.

And to the gracious people at Legacy—thank you for putting my passion on the printed page.

FOREWORD

This is a book of vision. Don't get me wrong, it is emphatically practical, eminently readable, and immediately accessible. This is not another tome of high falutin' ivory tower stuff. It is sane, sound, and sensible. Even so, its most notable feature is its unswerving vision of what the church can be—and indeed, what the church ought to be.

Sadly, vision is a commodity in rather short supply these days. In all too many cases it has been supplanted in modern ministry by mere mechanical formulas or lowest common denominators. A tidal wave of steely and institutional pragmatism—driven along by the fierce winds of marketing concerns, demographic data, bureaucratic models, and corporate efficiency standards—has very nearly engulfed the sensibility for passionate vision in the church. This is especially true in women's ministry, where the tides of time and circumstance seem to roil in a perpetual storm of turbulence and confusion. And "where there is no vision, the people perish" (Proverbs 29:18).

But a reassertion of vision—a steadfast Biblical vision—can calm those raucous waters. It can still the stormy sea of theological ambivalence. This book has grown out of that kind of vision.

For the last two decades, Susan Hunt has modeled for the church what a true disciple should be. She has demonstrated, in both word and deed that such a vision of faithful service is the only vision that can adequately meet the pressing needs all around us. In this book, she shares with us the detailed innerworkings and under-pinnings of that vision.

Susan gently and skillfully reminds us that there are no quick fixes, no magic formulas, and no instant cures for the ills of our time. There is no easy way to effectively equip women to grow into maturity in Christ. Instead she says that the very essence of women's ministry—and in fact all ministry—is interpersonal. It is women mentoring women. It is older women caring for younger women—teaching, nurturing, and encouraging them. She draws on a wealth of Scriptural material to illumine the righteous and venerable tradition of people actually investing themselves in people—rather than in programs, projects, or perspectives.

That is truly visionary. And, it is oh so needed in this angst-ridden world of ours.

Nearly a century ago, the great Theodore Roosevelt issued forth with a clarion cry:

> Do we see as we ought to see? Do we see the warrior witnesses round about us—or are we like the servants of Elisha, purblind and incognizant of the battle raging in our midst? Do we see the Savior before us—or are we like the disciples on the way to Emmaus, obsessed and possessed by our own concerns? Do we see—or are we casting about in darkness, flailing with sightless eyes? With what encumbrances have we ballasted the Gospel of grace with our lack of vision? Surely the Kingdom of Righteousness does not lack for resources. Surely the church is not bereft of ingenuity. Surely the just have bounteous opportunities. Yea and indeed, the single and solitary need—of the hour, the day, the epoch—is vision: the vision to see, the vision to do, and more, the vision to be. Lord of the Harvest, give us we pray: great men, great women, and great families. Lord of the Harvest, give us we pray: vision—the vision of gallant greatness.

This book is a response to just such a cry. To it I can only add my heartiest amen.

GEORGE GRANT
Franklin, Tennessee

INTRODUCTION

For several years I had a suspicion that Titus 2:3–5 contained exciting principles and implications for women. I had theories about the benefits of older-women/younger-women relationships, but I had few contemporary examples that validated my theories.

My husband was pastor of a wonderful church, but it consisted primarily of young families. Even though I was only in my late thirties to late forties during that time, I was an "older woman." The three or four older women who came into our fellowship gave me occasional glimpses of what I thought Titus 2:3–5 should look like, but then I would hear of an example that contradicted my theories.

In my work as consultant for the Women In the Church ministries for our denomination, I frequently have calls from pastors telling me about tension between the older and younger women in their churches. I knew that it should work because God said to do it, but I had no models to show me how it should work. The commentaries which I searched for more information seemed to slide by that portion of Scripture with little comment except that God said older women should teach younger women—and I already knew that!

But why wasn't it working in individual relationships and in churches? What were the missing pieces? What did older women and younger women need to know to obey this command? My growing conviction was that the Titus principle held something rich and wonderful for women, but how to make it happen was fuzzy.

Then I came face to face with what Titus 2:3–5 looks like in action.

My husband went on staff of a church that has a rich blend of older and younger people. Since one of his responsibilities is evangelism, he asked me to begin a weekly Bible study for women that could serve as an outreach to our community and as a vehicle to help new women in the church develop friendships. The first week, I was stunned when many of the older women in the church appeared with their Bible in hand and an eagerness to be a part of this new program. I was expecting, and had prepared for, six or seven young women who had been visiting the church. Now sitting before me were women in their sixties and seventies whose knowledge of and experience with the Holy One far exceeded my own. I had to do some mental gymnastics, and some quick praying, to adapt. How do you teach women in their twenties and women in their seventies— and everything in between!

Soon I realized that God was giving me an opportunity to "prove Him right" regarding the Titus principle. But I also realized that I had to help the women build bridges across the generations. We had to learn to relate on a deep level. We had to learn how to learn from one another. A turning point came when I felt led of the Lord to teach a lesson on marriage. *But Lord*, I argued, *how can I do that when so many of the women in our group are widows? I know the younger women need it, but won't it be too painful for the widows?*

As I continued praying, the answer became clear: *The widows are your most valuable resource in teaching this lesson.* Equally clear was the knowledge that I couldn't expect the widows to see themselves as a resource—that would be part of the teaching process.

So I began the lesson by sharing my questions to the Lord and His answer to me. Then I asked the older women, including the widows, to freely share their memories and insights with us. During the small group discussion times, these wonderful older women opened their hearts to the younger women. When a younger woman said, "How can I possibly go home and complain about dirty socks on the floor after hearing these women share their precious memories about their husbands," I knew that I had seen the Titus principle work.

And I have seen it grow and deepen in many practical ways. Months later, when the group was sharing the benefits of older-women/younger-women relationships, the younger women talked of the many things they had learned from the older women. But again I knew we had experienced what God desires when the older women talked of how they had learned from the

---

The combination of younger women who are teachable and godly older women who are willing to open their hearts gave us the privilege of obeying the Titus mandate.

---

younger women. They particularly talked of how they had learned to communicate more openly and to share their feelings with the younger women.

My observation is that the combination of younger women who are teachable and godly older women who are willing to open their hearts gave us the privilege of obeying the Titus mandate.

These older women in our Bible study are my heroines—they have made a deep impression on my life. I would like to tell you about one of them who epitomized all of them. Of all the women, I have chosen this particular one because just last week she was transferred from the church militant to the church triumphant, and I have spent a lot of time since then reflecting on her life.

Mrs. Elizabeth Scott, known affectionately as "Miss" Elizabeth, was 76. She was a quiet, humble woman who did not have a high-profile ministry, yet the church was packed for her funeral. The hundreds of people who attended were deeply moved by her death. I was particularly struck by my conversations with the women. I thought that Miss Elizabeth was my special encourager—my personal fan club—my cheerleader. Since knowing her, I have had more confidence to assume responsibilities because I knew she was in my corner praying and cheering me on. What astounded me was that it seemed as if every woman there had the same relationship with her! She had done for them what she had done for me—yet it had been done in such a quiet way that we each thought we were her special project.

I simply could not believe the women who talked about their families being invited to a meal in her home, or those who told how she had invited them to our church, or how she had been the first person to greet them when they visited the church, or the women who talked about receiving cards and telephone calls from her.

As I have contemplated the power of her life, I have also been struck with what she did not do. Gossip, complaint, and criticism had no part in her life.

Miss Elizabeth loved the young women in the church. We often heard her say, "I'm so thankful for our young women. They are the ones who will carry on." Although we have decided that none of us can fill her shoes, we are determined to collectively work together to fill the huge vacuum created by her death. She showed us what women in a local church should be. She left us a precious legacy.

At her funeral, my husband read Proverbs 31. A reverent awe fell over the congregation as each verse was read because we realized that here was an accurate description of this godly woman. Other Proverbs 31 women, such as Elisabeth Elliot and Edith Schaeffer are also my heroines; however, they are "comfortable" heroines because I can excuse myself for not measuring up to who and what they are. As I stand before the memory of Miss Elizabeth, I feel some discomfort because I have no excuse. But I also feel challenged because what she was and what she did, any Christian woman can be and do. She had no extraordinary gifts or circumstances. She simply loved Jesus and lived each day for His glory. She imitated Him by serving those around her.

Her son expressed it well: "No verbal defense could ever validate the gospel like Mama's life of love did."

She was what I want to be: the essence of a spiritual mother. It is because women like Miss Elizabeth have been willing to enter into nurturing relationships with younger women, to encourage and equip them to live for God's glory, that I have had the privilege of seeing Titus 2:3–5 in action. My theories have not only been validated, they have also been expanded beyond anything I could have imagined; I now have a passion to see the Titus principle operative in the lives of Christian women.

Any woman reading this book can begin to reach out and develop spiritual mother-daughter relationships, but I encourage you to use this as a group study. The Titus command is given to the church. It can best be implemented in the church through a relevant women's ministry. The Leader's Guide for this book gives suggestions for group study and exercises to help a group implement the Titus principle.[1]

I have written the words in this book, but the women of Midway Presbyterian Church (PCA) have lived the words. They have translated Biblical truth into vibrant relationships. They are my heroines.

PART ONE

THE MANDATE

*You must teach what is in accord
with sound doctrine. Teach the older men
to be temperate, worthy of respect, self-controlled,
and sound in faith, in love and in endurance.
Likewise, teach the older women
to be reverent in the way they live,
not to be slanderers or addicted to much wine,
but to teach what is good. Then they can train the
younger women to love their husbands and children,
to be self-controlled and pure,
to be busy at home, to be kind, and
to be subject to their husbands,
so that no one will malign
the word of God.*

Titus 2:1–5

Julie's Story

I went to the Health Care Center with the idea that I was going to encourage some of the elderly patients. It happened the other way around. I was the one who was encouraged because of time spent with a wise woman of the Lord.

I had never met Mrs. Johnson, but conversation came easily. Soon she told me that she felt there was no purpose for living anymore, and she wished the Lord would take her to Himself. Then our conversation shifted to the Lord. As we talked about His faithfulness and His sovereignty, Mrs. Johnson agreed that since she was still here, the Lord had a reason for it. She began talking about her gratitude for God's care throughout her life. She told me how she had become a Christian and changed her lifestyle, and how she had prayed for her husband and her mother for many years and then seen the Lord work in their hearts and draw them to Himself.

As she told story after story of God's working in her life, I was reminded of God's faithfulness to His people. I saw in Mrs. Johnson a loyal and obedient servant, one who had humbled herself in order to give God the glory in her life. As I listened, I became aware that I had discovered a treasure: A present-day godly role model of Christian womanhood that is a rarity in this day and age. As she spoke of her husband, she exhorted me to love my husband. When I told her I was excited about having children and that I wanted to stay at home with them, she beamed and told me that was the most important thing I could do. What unusual advice to receive in this illustrious, modern age of the 1990s! This was an encouragement to me, a young woman seeking to please the Lord in a society that says "fulfill your-self" and "demand your rights."

An hour had passed, and Mrs. Johnson apologized for talking so long. She seemed surprised when I told her what a blessing she had been to me.

What a pity that this godly woman, with a lifetime's store of wisdom, lives a lonely and secluded life with no one even acknowledging, much less benefiting from, her treasure of knowledge. When I left, we were both smiling. She had been of value to someone, and I had gained precious wisdom. A simple Biblical principle had been put into practice, and God had blessed it. The Titus principle tells older women to train and encourage younger women. Too often today, older women are an untapped resource in our churches, while younger women are searching for Proverbs 31 women whom they can emulate. God's answer solves both problems.

Julie Garland
St. Louis, Missouri

1

OUR REFERENCE POINT

O Jerusalem, Jerusalem . . .
how often I have longed to gather your children together,
as a hen gathers her chicks under her wings.

Matthew 23:37

T he teenager was unmarried and pregnant. She had experienced incredible emotional highs and lows during the last
several days. As she stood at the front door of an older woman
relative, she wondered what her reaction would be. She knew
what rejection felt like. She remembered her fiancé's reaction
and the events which caused him to changed his mind. Would
her friend reject her?

We don't know what emotions were swirling inside Mary as
she raised her hand to knock on the door. But we do know that
less than five minutes inside that door, she experienced a joy
and confidence unexpected in one so young. Only a few moments in Elizabeth's presence and Mary burst into a magnificent
song of praise to God, recorded for us in Luke 1:46–55.

What happened between these two women is the essence of
spiritual mothering. When women do for other women what
Elizabeth did for Mary, I believe we will see young women burst
forth in lives of praise to God. And that is the goal of spiritual
mothering.

The American Heritage Dictionary of the English Language
gives the following definitions:

mother: a female that has borne an offspring. A female who has adopted a child or otherwise established a maternal relationship with another person.

mothering: to give birth to . . . to create and care for; instigate and carry through. To watch over, nourish, and protect.

Based on this definition, my working definition for the spiritual mothering relationship is this:

When a woman possessing faith and spiritual maturity enters into a nurturing relationship with a younger woman in order to encourage and equip her to live for God's glory.

Please note that giving birth biologically or being of a certain chronological age are not prerequisites for spiritual mothering.

Our Model for This Relationship

Though powerful examples, Elizabeth and Mary are not the ultimate reference point for spiritual mothering. "In the beginning God created" is both a fact of history and a principle for life. God is the source of life and the model for living life. A proper approach to any situation or topic begins with God. To use God as the reference point for the topic of spiritual mothering is not an attempt to feminize God. It is simply an attempt to relate all of life to Him.

God's relationship with His people forms the pinnacle for the spiritual mothering concept defined above. Nurturing His people through His Word and by His Spirit, the Triune God enters into a covenant relationship. He is both the source and the sustainer of physical and spiritual life. One Hebrew name of God, *El Shaddai*, provides a window for us to understand how He relates to His people.

The traditional translations of Scripture have consistently rendered this name "Almighty." But to appreciate its full flavor, it will be helpful to examine its Hebrew roots. *El* is a shortened form of *Elohim*. It sets forth the might, the strength, and the excellence of God. *Shad* is the Hebrew word for breast. *Shaddai* pictures God's fullness or bounty, his tenderness, his generosity, his desire to nurture us and make us fruitful. In one name, God's attributes of might and tenderness are brought together![1]

Another dimension of this nurturing relationship is described by the prophet Isaiah:

Can a mother forget the baby at her breast and have no compassion on the child she has borne? Though she may forget, I will not forget you! See, I have engraved you on the palms of my hands. . . . (Isaiah 49:15–16a)

In this passage, God encourages believers not to lose hope in the midst of difficulties and gives us a message of comfort. John Calvin noted the Lord used the comparison to a mother's love to convey His anxiety about His people, a love "so strong

---

When women do for other women what Elizabeth did for Mary, I believe we will see young women burst forth in lives of praise to God.

---

and ardent, as to leave far behind it a father's love." He goes further in declaring He would never forget His children for His love "is far stronger and warmer than the love of all mothers." Calvin concludes with this: "In a word, the Prophet here describes to us the inconceivable carefulness with which God unceasingly watches over our salvation, that we may be fully convinced that he will never forsake us, though we may be afflicted with great and numerous calamities."[2]

Through the prophet Isaiah, the Lord again used the mother metaphor:

Rejoice with Jerusalem and be glad for her, all you who love her; rejoice greatly with her, all you who mourn over her. For

you will nurse and be satisfied at her comforting breasts; you
will drink deeply and delight in her overflowing abundance.
. . . I will extend peace to her like a river, and the wealth of
nations like a flooding stream; you will nurse and be carried
on her arm and dandled on her knees. As a mother comforts
her child, so will I comfort you; and you will be comforted
over Jerusalem. When you see this, your heart will rejoice
and you will flourish like grass. (Isaiah 66:10–14a)

This passage is a discourse on true and false worship. It is
designed to warn and fortify true worshippers for the grief they
will endure from the hypocritical worshippers. Though the immediate context is to the Jews upon their return from captivity,
the prophecy also looked ahead to the establishment of the gospel church and the terror God would bring upon the enemies of
that church. In order to assure the true worshippers of his deep
affection and protection, the Lord compares Himself and the
church to a mother. The person who experiences this motherly
affection and protection rejoices and flourishes.

And then in the New Testament we have the piercing pa-
thos of the words of Jesus as he looked over Jerusalem:

O Jerusalem, Jerusalem, you who kill the prophets and stone
those sent to you, how often I have longed to gather your
children together, as a hen gathers her chicks under her
wings, but you were not willing. (Matthew 23:37)

Jesus unabashedly displays his compassion and tenderness
for those who had rejected him. He uses the illustration of a
hen to explain his intense desire to protect them. Whenever
danger approaches, a mother hen quickly gathers her chicks
under her wings and sits on them. Even if the impending danger threatens her life, her chicks will be protected. The re-
spected preacher John MacArthur, in writing about this
passage, said: "The Lord's illustration depicts His great tenderness. He didn't speak to Israel merely in theological terms; He
spoke to the people in a personal, intimate way. He wanted to
give them security."[3]

Our Capacity for Mothering

The name *El Shaddai* and Scripture surely give value to mothering, but they also imply a capacity for mothering that has been given to women. Biological birthing is not the activator of this capacity; women who have never given physical birth still have this mothering capacity and can exhibit mothering characteristics.

The development of this mothering capacity is affected by instinct and learning but is hindered by sin. When the Holy Spirit produces faith in a woman, she becomes a new creation (2 Corinthians 5:17). A dramatic result of her newness is her even greater potential for the development of this female capacity. The Christian woman not only has a new Pattern, she has a new Power.

As a woman's growing desire to imitate God produces obedience to His Word, she develops mothering characteristics. Our femaleness gives us the capacity for mothering; our faith produces certain characteristics of mothering. Some characteristics we see from the Scriptures are strength, excellence, tenderness, generosity, desire to nurture, comfort, compassion, affection, protection, and sacrifice. These characteristics are relational—they simply will not allow a person to be an isolationist. The posses-

---

> ### *The Christian woman not only has a new Pattern; she has a new Power.*

---

sion of these characteristics creates an intense desire to nurture and to be nurtured. The results in the recipients are security and fruitfulness. They will flourish like grass.

Consider the relationship between Ruth and Naomi—an impressive illustration of spiritual mothering. In this Old Testament story, we see two women who had bonded! Naomi must have done something right to have elicited such commitment from her daughter-in-law.

When famine struck Israel, Naomi, her husband, and two sons moved to Moab. The sons married Moabite women. After the death of her husband and sons, Naomi decided to return to Judah. She encouraged her daughters-in-law to return to their mother's homes; however, Ruth chose to remain with Naomi. At this juncture in the story, Naomi appears to be hopeless and bitter, yet Ruth insisted on following her. Why was Ruth so determined to follow a seemingly hopeless, bitter woman?

Apparently Ruth had seen the real Naomi. It was unacceptable for an Israelite to marry a Moabite, yet Ruth must have felt Naomi's acceptance. Ruth must have heard of Jehovah and seen the reality of Him in the life of Naomi's family. Perhaps she observed the hope that sustained Naomi through the death of her husband and sons. This reality of Naomi's faith caused Ruth to tenaciously cling to her. When Ruth says, "Don't urge me to leave you . . . Where you go I will go. . . . Your people will be my people and your God my God," you feel her determination to be identified with the God of Israel (Ruth 1:16). The bond between them was their common commitment to Jehovah. These women had the same reference point.

They returned to Israel. Ruth worked in the fields. Naomi remained at home. Naomi was probably too old for the physical work, but each night she encouraged and equipped Ruth—a fundamental principle of spiritual mothering. Often younger women tell me that the older women in their church aren't willing to spiritually mother. I ask them to elaborate. "We've asked them to teach our Bible study so that we can learn from them and none of them are willing." My reply is, "You're asking for the wrong thing. You're asking them to go out into the fields rather than encourage and equip you to go." Ruth was willing to listen to Naomi's advice and to follow her instructions—she was teachable.

Ultimately Naomi's emptiness was changed to fullness. Ruth married Boaz and they had a son. When Ruth's baby was born, the Israelite women said to Naomi, "'Praise be to the

LORD, who this day has not left you without a kinsman-redeemer. May he become famous throughout Israel. He will renew your life and sustain you in your old age. For your daughter-in-law, who loves you and who is better to you than seven sons, has given him birth.' Then Naomi took the child, laid him in her lap and cared for him" (Ruth 4:14–15).

Indeed, this son did become famous throughout Israel. He was the grandfather of David, and Ruth's name appears in Matthew's genealogy of Jesus.

An older woman cultivated a nurturing relationship with a younger woman. The younger woman was willing to listen and to heed the advice, though sometimes it must have sounded strange. And the result was that these women are bound up in the very life of the Messiah.

In the spiritual mothering story at the beginning of this chapter, Julie Garland told of meeting Mrs. Johnson in a nursing home. As the two women talked, Mrs. Johnson expressed feelings of uselessness. She could not understand why she was still living. She saw no purpose or hope in her life. Then Julie asked questions about her faith, and simply rehearsing the goodness of the Lord in her life refreshed Mrs. Johnson.

Since Julie told me this story a year ago, I recently received an update. Julie and Mrs. Johnson have become close friends. Julie visits her once a week since Mrs. Johnson has no living family. She spent Thanksgiving with Julie and her husband. "I am expecting a baby in June," writes Julie. "Mrs. Johnson is encouraging me to be a godly mother. She never had children of her own and is very excited about the baby. On my last visit, Mrs. Johnson had some exciting news. The night before she led her roommate to the Lord! I talked with this new believer and she had a good understanding of the gospel, which is no surprise with Mrs. Johnson as her teacher."

Mrs. Johnson's words to Julie were these: "I believe this is the reason God has kept me alive this long!"

Mrs. Johnson will be eighty-five on her next birthday, and she is currently discipling her roommate and continuing to spiritually mother Julie.

Julie and her husband will graduate from Covenant Theological Seminary in May. Julie has received a wonderful education in the seminary classrooms, but I suspect she would agree
with me that the lessons she has learned in Mrs. Johnson's
room have been just as valuable.

A simple visit to a nursing home—something anyone can
do. And yet the lives of two, and now three, women have been
enriched.

Our Need for Mothering

Countless women today long to be nurtured. They want the love
and acceptance of a mother or a mother-substitute. They want
to feel the warmth and security of an older woman's approval.
And countless women of faith throughout the world today are
the embodiment of these and other virtues that equip them to
nurture younger women. But they don't know how to do it.

The eighteenth century poet and historian, Matthew Arnold, said: "If ever the world sees a time when women shall
come together purely and simply for the benefit and good of
mankind, it will be a power such as the world has never seen."[4] I
agree. But the problem is that women will never come together
purely and simply for the benefit and good of others because of
the self-centeredness of our sin nature. The what's-in-it-for-me
mentality forbids such selflessness. However, Christian women,
because of the power of grace, can overcome their self-centeredness. Christian women can manifest the other-centered virtues
that characterize spiritual mothering. In fact, I would restate
Matthew Arnold in this way: If ever the world sees a time when
Christian women shall come together purely and simply to encourage and equip other women to live for God's glory, it will be
a power such as the world has never seen.

I am deeply impressed by the excellence of Christian
women around the world whom I have had the privilege to
meet and/or observe. These women believe God's Word is the
only infallible rule for faith and practice, and they are committed
to living out God's truth in the daily occurrences of their lives.

Christian women are committed to making a difference for Jesus in this generation.

These women believe in and live by prayer. Their social consciences have been shaped by God's truth, and they are committed to making a difference for Jesus in this generation. They believe that the church is the bride of Christ and have committed themselves to serve Him through their local fellowships.

These women stand in stark contrast to the image of womanhood that is being flaunted today. As I observe these women, I wonder if perhaps we are on the verge of seeing their power unleashed—the power of grace in the lives of godly women influencing families, churches, communities, our nation, and the world—influencing not with clenched fists, but with open arms.

I believe with all my heart that there is the potential for a revival of faith and virtue among women. If Christian women begin to fathom the power of our God-given capacity, develop these God-honoring characteristics, and nurture younger women, perhaps we will see the fruit of righteousness flourish in women in our decade.

We have clearly been given the model for spiritual mothering. The command is just as clear:

> Likewise, teach the older women to be reverent in the way they live, not to be slanderers or addicted to much wine, but to teach what is good. Then they can train the younger women to love their husbands and children, to be self-controlled and pure, to be busy at home, to be kind, and to be subject to their husbands, so that no one will malign the word of God. (Titus 2:3–5)

Jesus tells us that those who love Him will keep His commandments. What He commands us to do, He enables us to do. Join me as we explore how women of faith are to obey this command.

🐝   🐝   🐝

A Spiritual Mothering Challenge

1. Begin with a season of prayer.

   a. Read Matthew 23:37. If you have trusted the sacrificial death of Jesus in your place, praise Him for your salvation. If you have not, I urge you to cast yourself on His mercy and trust in Him alone for salvation.

   b. Read Isaiah 49:14–16a. Thank God for the compassion He has shown to you and for the security of knowing that you are engraved on the palms of His hands.

   c. Read Isaiah 66:10–14a. Thank God for His comfort. Pray that your heart will rejoice in Him and that you will flourish spiritually.

   d. Meditate on Colossians 1:16–18.

2. Is God your reference point? Does He have supremacy in your life? If so, you have much to offer a younger woman. Begin praying for an opportunity. Also, seek out an older woman who displays this kind of focus in her life and learn from her.

3. Write a card to an older and/or younger woman and express your appreciation for her.

4. Do you have a ministry that you could share with an older or younger woman? If you visit a local nursing home, work in a crisis pregnancy center, or visit an elderly relative, invite an older or younger woman to go along with you. If you don't have a ministry, find a woman who does and ask her if you can go with her.

Jerdone's Story

Early in my Christian life, the Lord instilled deep within my heart a vision for ministry. I knew that someday I would leave my much loved profession of nursing to follow God's next calling for me, spiritual motherhood—enabling women to ground themselves in God's Word. By encouraging women to grow in their love and knowledge of the Lord Jesus, I knew that they could balance all facets of their being. I knew this with a profound certainty because God was doing just that in me.

At that time, God gave me a bittersweet promise:

> "Sing, O barren woman, you who never bore a child; burst into song, shout for joy, you who were never in labor; because more are the children of the desolate woman than of her who has a husband," says the LORD. . . . "You will forget the shame of your youth and remember no more the reproach of your widowhood. For your Maker is your husband—the Lord Almighty is his name—the Holy One of Israel is your Redeemer; he is called the God of all the earth. . . .
>
> "All your sons will be taught by the Lord, and great will be your children's peace." (Isaiah 54:1, 4–6, 13)

Emotionally, I screamed a rejection letter to my sovereign Lord. I wanted a physical husband and five children of my own womb to fill my cozy nest that I would make for them. Many years have passed since that painful scream. In reflection, those years have been filled with God's tender presence, His leadership, His intimate love, and His zest for life. All of this He infused into me and exchanged my cry of barrenness for many precious spiritual children.

His promise became fact as He moved me from nursing to Bible teaching. Spiritually nurturing many college women through Bible study, prayer, and fellowship has made me a full-time mom. What a delight to see baby Christians grow into mature adults. May I introduce a few to you?

This first daughter reminds me of Abigail in the Old Testament. Abigail means a father's joy. The Lord introduced me to His plump, healthy baby when she was a freshman at the university. She had been fed the rich milk of God's Word. As a result she was happy and content. Wrapped in the blankets of our ministry she began to hunger for the meat of God's Word. As she and I have rejoiced together in God's faithfulness, I am seeing a beautiful godly woman step out of those blankets. The Lord has blessed her with wisdom, compassion, joy, a fresh energy for service, as well as with an unusual insight into people. He has also gifted her in the art of teaching His Word. Her heart is that of a discipler as she reaches out to younger women hungering for the same spiritual food. Not only is she her father's joy, but mine as well.

My brazenly outspoken child of the faith, Miriam, has been a picture of Moses and Aaron's sister of Biblical times. She longed to see others come to know Christ personally as she had done. Her approach was well-meaning but condemning; she was mistaken as a busybody instead of a compassionate friend. Many times my interpretation of her uninvited counsel was a gentle reminder: "Miriam, you are not the Holy Spirit." This rough gem blessed by God with the gift of evangelism needed to be planed, sanded, and polished. For four years she and I cried tears of oil on her rough stony areas, as the Holy Spirit delicately positioned the rasp to make her shine for Him. Her zeal for evangelism is emerging as a clear, sparkling eye-catcher which reflects God's glory to a dark world. In her heart of hearts, she sees God's glory shimmering from the prism of her life on the foreign mission field.

Another daughter I have named Zoar because she reminded me of Lot's wife, a woman who remained nameless in Scripture. Zoar means small and this child represents a small mirror to me. Sometimes our children in their rebellion wander far from home. This mirror of me caused my heart to ache as I saw her repeat the sins of my youth. She stayed close as long as I pampered her, but when I spoke truth, she bolted. The last I heard of her, she was still rebelling, having allowed her dreams of being a godly woman slide to the bottom of her priorities. She looked back rather than heeded the warnings issued to her. As the Lord prompts me, I pray. It took the Holy Spirit nine years to woo me to Himself. I know the power of someone's prayer. My mirror, Zoar, will know as well.

Deborah was an administrative leader in Israel, and this daughter reminds me of Deborah as her spiritual gifts have sharpened during her growing years. This shy, soft spoken non-Christian began meeting with me weekly to study Scripture. She developed a solid relationship with the Lord, and her hunger for Bible study consistently grew in proportion to her Christian maturity. Now bold in writing and speech, she stands up for Christ in the secular university classrooms. The opposition she faces does not thwart her but rather challenges her. The Lord is developing sound muscle-tone in her for the spiritual battleground. She knows her Victor, Jesus; therefore, she is not afraid of her defeated foe when he groans.

These few cameo shots are from the larger family portrait which the Lord has hung in my home. I remember Isaiah 54:1: " . . . 'For the children of the desolate one will be more numerous than the children of the married woman,' says the LORD." I rejoice in His promise and in His faithfulness to perform that for me.

M. Jerdone Davis
Clemson, South Carolina

2

A LIFE-PURPOSE

I am the Lord's servant.
. . . May it be to me as you have said.

Luke 1:38

T he starting point in our discussion of spiritual mothering
was God; He is our reference point, the model for all of
life. This is our first foundational principle.

The second pivotal principle is that we have been created
to glorify God. This life-purpose is the driving force of our spiritual mothering definition:

> When a woman possessing faith and spiritual maturity enters
> into a relationship with a younger woman in order to encour-
> age and equip her to live for God's glory.

The relationship is not the driving force of spiritual mothering—God's glory is the premier purpose. So obviously, we need
to examine what it means to live for God's glory.

Ultimately, God Himself is again our model. God is glorious
in and of Himself. He does not need for us to glorify Him in
order for Him to be glorified. The Father, Son, and Holy Spirit
glorify one another:

> [Jesus prayed,] "Father, the time has come. Glorify your Son,
> that your Son may glorify you." (John 17:1)

> But when he, the Spirit of truth, comes, he will guide you
> into all truth. . . . He will bring glory to me by taking from
> what is mine and making it known to you. (John 16:13–14)

25

Jesus replied, "If I glorify myself, my glory means nothing. My Father, whom you claim as your God, is the one who glorifies me." (John 8:54)

Jesus tells us in no uncertain terms how to glorify God: "I have brought you glory on earth by completing the work you gave me to do . . ." (John 17:4).

Completing the work He assigns us—joyful obedience to His will—is the way we glorify Him. Through obedience, we reflect the glory of the glorious One. Glorifying God is the very essence of the Christian life. Mary, the mother of the Messiah, is an example of a woman who translated that essence into her existence as a female.

I fear that too often we do not hold Mary up as an example, because we are overcompensating for some who have elevated her above humanity. This reaction robs us of one of the most beautiful examples of faith found in Scripture. Of course, she is not a perfect example. Only God Himself is the Perfect Example. But in Mary we do see a woman who embraced God's glory as her reason for being and translated that into her experiences.

No earthly relationship will meet all of our needs. Fulfilling the purpose for which we were created is the only way we will experience wholeness. Mary focused on glorifying God. She did not seek Elizabeth as her only source of help; spiritual mothering is not a cure-all for the older or the younger woman. Some women may read this book and only think about their intense need for a spiritual mother-daughter relationship. They may feel that if they had such a relationship, their problems would be solved. Then they will be disappointed and discouraged if such a relationship does not happen. And even if it does happen, it will not fully fill the vacuums in their souls. This book should not be read only from the perspective of your need. Please read it from the perspective of how you can glorify God by enriching the lives of other women as you encourage and equip them to glorify Him. One reason Mary is an appropriate example of a spiritual daughter is that she is first an example of someone who was intent on glorifying God. To glorify God means to reflect back to Him the glory He has revealed to us.

A Response of Faith

Suddenly, without warning, Mary was hurled from the quiet life of small town obscurity to a succession of emotional highs and lows. Consider the staggering extremes:

- astonishment at seeing an angel.
- exhilaration upon hearing that she had been chosen to carry the Son of God in her womb.
- anxiety about how her fiancé would accept such news.
- confusion concerning the legitimate question of how such a physical impossibility could take place since she was a virgin.
- fear of the possible consequences of rejection and shame.

Yet this young woman handled the situation without her brain or her emotions becoming scrambled. After hearing the angel's incredible announcement, her response was immediate and unequivocal: "I am the Lord's servant. . . . May it be to me as you have said."

The trust in this statement is almost childlike. Mary defined herself with startling simplicity: "I am the Lord's servant." She stated her life-purpose clearly: "May it be to me as you have said." Obedience to God's will was the driving force of her life.

She stated her life-purpose clearly: "May it be to me as you have said."

How did Mary attain such clarity of purpose at such a young age? If we miss this, we miss the fact that Mary was one of us and that what she possessed is available to us. I believe two factors led up to her faith-response.

First, Scripture tells us that Mary was the object of God's grace. When the angel appeared to her, his first statement was:

"Greetings, you who are highly favored! The Lord is with you" (Luke 1:28). The Greek word translated *favor* means "grace, kindness, to give freely." From the first the angel reminded Mary of the grace of God in her life. Neither her good works nor her outstanding abilities had prepared her for the mission of being the mother of the Messiah, but God's undeserved grace bestowed upon her was the power-source within her.

Second was the answer to Mary's question, "How will this be?" The angel stated the truth that was absolutely necessary in order for Mary to submit. "The Holy Spirit will come upon you, and the power of the Most High will overshadow you" (Luke 1:35).

Scripture often speaks of God's shadow over us in relation to His guarding and protecting us: "Keep me as the apple of your eye, hide me in the shadow of your wings from the wicked who assail me, from my mortal enemies who surround me" (Psalm 17:8–9).

God's power in her and His protection over her were clearly presented. It was then that Mary could respond, "I am the Lord's servant." This was no emotional reaction but rather a deliberate and logical response based upon the character and the promises of God. Submission to such a mission would have been foolish otherwise.

Mary, like most women today, was a woman who experienced extraordinary extremes. And the extremes did not end when the angel left for his heavenly destination. Her continued ability to handle the extremes was because the core issue of her life-purpose was settled when the angel confronted her with God's sovereign love and power.

Consider the thrill of running to tell the man of her dreams about her wonderful news—only to be met with his devastating rejection. Joseph did not believe her! The wedding was off. It took an angel from God to convince him that she had not been unfaithful. Then the wedding was on again. Extremes! Was she not plagued with pride, resentment, and anger? Perhaps so, but desire for God's glory implies yielding to His way of ordering people and events. Even during the interlude between the off and on status of the wedding, she must have remained focused on the power of the Most High. She knew she did not have to convince Joseph; that was God's business. And as always, God's way was better. Obviously, God wanted Joseph to have an angelic experience. This would remove all doubt about the identity of the Child's father not only at that moment but in the years to come. And think of the fun Mary and Joseph must have had in being able to compare "angel stories." Anyone else would think they were crazy, but they could now share this experience with each other.

Clarity of Purpose

Then nine months later she found herself wandering the back alleys of Bethlehem on a donkey. She was about to give birth, and Joseph could not find a place for them to stay. Remember what she had been told:

> You have found favor with God. You will be with child and give birth to a son, . . . the Son of the Most High. The Lord God will give him the throne of his father David, and he will reign over the house of Jacob forever; his kingdom will never end. (Luke 1:30–33)

Now I must admit that if I heard an angel talking about the Son of the Most High, thrones, reigning, and kingdoms, my expectations would run in the direction of palaces, riches, and fame. She was to give birth to a king. Couldn't she at least expect a palace? I wonder if each time they turned a corner she expected someone to recognize them and lead them to a mansion with a four-poster bed and silk sheets.

Yet she was eventually faced with the reality: This King in her womb would be born in a stable. What inappropriate extremes! We have romanticized the "manger scene," but I have yet to see a stable where I would want to spend a night, much less give birth.

And then there was the visit by some men who said that angels announced the birth of her child to them. How could there be such an angelic celebration when she was stuck in a stable with donkeys and goats?

A celebration and a stable—two extremes:

> And all who heard it were amazed . . . but Mary treasured up all these things and pondered them in her heart. (Luke 2:18–19)

Everyone else was amazed. The extremes didn't make sense. But Mary treasured every aspect of the event; she did not treat her experiences carelessly. She wanted to squeeze every lesson out of each moment. Apparently she was not disappointed because her expectations had not been realized. Apparently she was not distracted by the sights and sounds of crowded Bethlehem or by the discomfort of giving birth in a stable or by the adulation of the shepherds. She exercised the discipline necessary to move beyond disappointments and distractions and to carefully think about the thing that really mattered—God's glory.

Again we have to wonder how Mary, in spite of her youth and her less-than-desirable circumstances, was able to demonstrate such clarity of purpose. What did she know that everyone else seems not to have known? Why was she not on stress-overload with these extremes in her life?

Mary heard the "kingdom-talk" of the angel. But she also heard the rest of the angel's message: *"You are to give him the name Jesus."*

Jesus means Savior. Throughout the Old Testament salvation and sacrifice were inseparably linked. To be the Savior meant that He would be the Lamb—the Lamb who would be sacrificed for the sins of His people. Mary knew the covenant promises, but she also knew the covenant conditions. As Joseph frantically tried to find a place for them to stay in Bethlehem, and someone offered a stable, I wonder if the lights came on for Mary. I can imagine her reaction, *Of course, where else would a lamb be born except in a stable! Lord, you think of everything!*

Some would think it sad and degrading that the King of Glory was born in a stable. But it was the obvious place for the Lamb of God to be born. So the stable and the angelic celebration were not incompatible from God's perspective. Mary could adjust to these extremes in her life because she saw them from

---

In defining herself as a servant, Mary had relinquished control to God. Her purpose was not her convenience but God's glory.

---

the vantage point of obeying God's will, not from the perspective of her expectations or preferences. In defining herself as a servant, she had relinquished control to God. Her purpose was not her convenience but God's glory.

Mary's response is beautiful, but it does not compare with the beauty of God's grace and the power of His sovereignty. And Mary knew this. Her song to Elizabeth tells us that she was under no illusions about her own ability or position:

> My soul glorifies the Lord and my spirit rejoices in God my Savior, for He has been mindful of the humble state of His servant. From now on all generations will call me blessed, for the Mighty One has done great things for me—holy is his name. (Luke 1:46–49)

Her heart was joyful because God had been mindful of her. Out of His sovereign grace He had looked upon her. When she talked about her humble state, it was not false or pretended humility but an honest conviction of her condition apart from God's saving grace. This absence of pride or pretense freed Mary to say, "May it be to me as you have said." And think of the Treasure she received in that stable!

A Life of Obedience

Notice again the two factors that led to Mary's response. God's grace in her meant that He entered into a relationship with her. He poured His undeserved love into her. He accepted her as His own. God's protection over her was not an empty claim because this promise was made by the Most High. He could deliver that which He promised. Servitude makes no sense apart from these truths, but it makes perfect sense in light of them.

As a servant, Mary's agenda was simple—obedience to her Master. And we have already seen that loving obedience is the way we glorify God. Jesus said to His Father, "I have brought you glory on earth by completing the work you gave me to do" (John 17:4).

Transferring ownership to Him rid her of such self-centered characteristics as self-promotion and self-interest. That's why there was a childlike composure about her. This confidence was appealing, not offensive, because it was not *self*-confidence. Mary's confidence was grounded in her relationship with God.

Many women today are overwhelmed with the complexity of life. They are floundering because they have no focal point. When their expectations are not realized, their emotional equilibrium erupts. When career, marriage, or children do not give them the security or significance they anticipated, their confidence evaporates. They are influenced by the unrealistic images of life and womanhood portrayed in the media. Their purpose in life is shaped by their desire to attain the personal happiness they are told they deserve. So they are not only disappointed by unrealized expectations, they are defeated. Christian women are not immune to this. A four-letter word causes us enormous problems: *self*. Our self-inclination will send us reeling unless we have settled that core issue: what is our life-purpose? Once God's glory is our purpose, then we have a center point to which we can relate each decision and each situation.

Servitude simplifies life.

Servitude is not easy. Obedience is not a one-time decision. Obedience is a life-time discipline. But it does bring a simplicity to life because it settles the issue of who is in control. It enables

---

For many women today, their purpose in life is shaped by their desire to attain the personal happiness they are told they deserve. So they are not only disappointed by unrealized expectations, they are defeated.

---

us to decode the confusing events in our lives. When a woman is absorbed with God's glory, she will interpret her life according to His truth.

God's grace enables us to know our mission in life and empowers us to fulfill our mission. When by His grace we behold His glory, then we know that the only reasonable purpose for our existence is to reflect that glory. When we experience God's grace and make the decision to glorify Him, then our soul will rejoice in God, regardless of our circumstances.

When we see Jesus as the Lamb of God, the One who sacrificed His life that we might have life, and we transfer ownership to Him, there is reason for celebration. The extremes make sense when viewed from the perspective of a Sovereign God who is navigating our circumstances to bring about His perfect plan. The "stables" are cause for celebration because it is the "stable experiences" that bring stability. It is the "stable experiences" that bring treasures:

> Consider it pure joy, my brothers [and sisters], whenever you face trials of many kinds, because you know that the testing of your faith develops perseverance. Perseverance must finish

its work so that you may be mature and complete, not lacking anything. (James 1:2–4)

And we know that in all things God works for the good of those who love him, who have been called according to his purpose. For those God foreknew he also predestined to be conformed to the likeness of his Son. (Romans 8:28–29)

Here we see Mary as a spiritual mother because she encouraged and equipped other women to live for God's glory. A woman so consumed with God's glory could not do otherwise. I cannot prove what influence she had on her contemporaries, but I do know that women in all generations have "called her blessed" and have been influenced by her example. I am one of them.

ۿ   ۿ   ۿ

A Spiritual Mothering Challenge

1. Begin with prayer.

   a. Meditate on Psalm 86:12–13. The words *all* and *forever* in this verse are inclusive. They leave no room for self-centeredness. Ask God to strip you of anything that may be prohibiting you from realizing your exciting potential—to glorify the God of glory.

   b. Can you honestly say that you want God's glory to be your life-purpose? If so, you are ready for a spiritual mother-daughter relationship. Ask the Lord to prepare you for and direct you to the relationship that will glorify Him. "Glorify the Lord with me; let us exalt his name together" (Psalm 34:3).

2. Write the statement "I am the Lord's servant" at the top of a piece of paper.

   a. Under that statement, list any hurts, expectations, disappointments, etc. that you are struggling with.

   b. Now ask God to enable you to interpret everything on your list in light of His will for you. Ask Him to show you how each person, circumstance, or event is your platform to reflect the glory of His grace that has been poured into you.

   c. Ask the Father to help you discover the treasure He has for you in your "stable."

Jane's Story

We hit Miami about the same time in the late 60's—the hippies and I.

We were looking for a place to be accepted. I'm not sure what the flower children found, but I discovered my niche through the women's ministry of the church we joined in Coral Gables.

What unusual women they were! They looked the same—many lived in mansions to my more modest-accustomed eyes, but there was a decided difference. I noticed it first when someone called, invited me to a women's Bible study, and even offered to come by to take me! The second thing I observed was how they talked. They talked a lot about Jesus. Then they prayed, and I knew for sure I was surrounded by a group of religious fanatics. These women, not just a few but all, poured out their hearts before the Lord, and I could detect tears bathing some of those prayers.

What had I gotten myself into? Could I get up and leave quietly and never visit this group again? Then, horror of horrors, I heard my own name mentioned. Someone I had never met before was praying for me out loud! This was a first. In all the years I had attended women's meetings in a variety of churches, no one had ever done such a thing. At first I was awash with embarrassment, but then my heart was warmed by this loving expression. I was thawing. Thus began my initiation into women ministering to other women.

The results were pretty wonderful. My life changed. A "neither hot nor cold" relationship with Jesus Christ turned into total commitment; prayers for my unsaved husband (something I had never been challenged to try before) resulted in a "new creature in Christ" spouse; our daughters grew spiritually, and within two years we had gone to seminary to embark on an adventure in faith that continues to this day.

This was twenty years ago. Is the ministry of women training women still valid today in the waning years of the twentieth century? I say a resounding "Yes and amen!" Perhaps more today than ever. The world buffets women on every side with a myriad of voices that confuse and distract. Strong ministries led by wise and godly women are needed to bring women to center-point, to offer Biblical solutions to the crises of life, and to provide nurturing, loving relationships.

Women reaching out to other women in the love of Christ—an unbeatable formula that results in eternal dividends.

Jane Brooks
Atlanta, Georgia

3

THE COMMAND

*Teach the older women to be reverent in the way they live,
not to be slanderers or addicted to much wine, but to teach
what is good. Then they can train the younger women.*

Titus 2:3–4

W e have established two foundational principles for
women of faith:

- God is the reference point for all of life.
- God's glory is the over-arching goal for all of life.

Now we are ready to explore the Titus mandate. In this
chapter we will consider the command itself.

This command is sandwiched between the exhortation to
"teach what is in accord with sound doctrine" (v. 1) and a
statement of purpose: "so that no one will malign the word of
God" (v. 5). Sound doctrine must be the basis for the older-
woman/younger-woman relationship and honor for God's truth
must be the goal of the relationship. This basis and this purpose
give the command its unique impetus.

Basis of the Command

Paul's instruction to Titus to teach the women morality based
on sound doctrine implies that the women were to be taught
doctrine. According to the *American Heritage Dictionary*, doc-

trine is "a creed of principles presented for acceptance or belief." The Greek word translated "sound" means safe, healthy.
So these women were to be taught the principles of the Christian faith which would form the basis for their character. The
soundness, or correctness, of the doctrine would give them a
foundation from which to train the younger women.

Sound doctrine qualifies the kind of morality Paul is advocating in the command. Morality must be based on who
God is and what He has done for us in Christ, or it will be
purely subjective. Unless God is the reference point, there is
no objective, absolute standard or authority for morality. If
we begin anywhere else, our morality will degenerate to the
level of the moral code of our environment. The virtues Paul
encourages "presuppose the dynamic of God's grace working
in the heart, and are motivated by the example of Christ, are
measured by God's holy law, and have God's glory as their
goal."[1]

Apparently Paul did not expect or want the women in
the Cretan church to change their conduct without changing
their thinking. He wanted them to think Christianly so that
they would act Christianly. And sound doctrine is essential
for right thinking. My impression from this is that Paul re-
garded these women as bright, perceptive individuals who
were capable of understanding doctrinal concepts. It would
seem that Paul did not expect these women to be given a
shallow approach to morality.

Sound doctrine will keep older women from being "tossed
back and forth by the waves, and blown here and there by
every wind of teaching and by the cunning and craftiness of
men in their deceitful scheming" (Ephesians 4:14). A well-
defined system of doctrine protects us from false teaching. It
also helps us maintain balance in the application of faith into
life. Sound doctrine keeps us on track and helps us avoid rigid
legalism and loose liberalism. Sound doctrine will produce the
stability that is essential for spiritual mothering.

Goal of the Command

The goal Paul gives for the older-woman/younger-woman relationship is a sober reminder that if our practice is inconsistent with our profession, we bring dishonor to that which we have professed. Honoring God's Word not only refers to the written Word (Holy Scripture), but also to the living Word (Jesus Christ):

> In the beginning was the Word, and the Word was with God, and the Word was God. . . . The Word became flesh and made his dwelling among us. We have seen his glory, the glory of the One and Only, who came from the Father, full of grace and truth. (John 1:1, 14)

To malign the Word is to malign God Himself. The Lord told Ezekiel that He dispersed the people of Israel because they defiled the land by their conduct, and that "wherever they went among the nations they profaned my holy name, for it was said of them, 'These are the LORD'S people, and yet they had to leave his land'" (Ezekiel 36:20–21). As people who are privileged to be called Christian, we must not allow our behavior—neither doing what is forbidden in the Word nor failing to do what is commanded in the Word—to desecrate the Name we bear.

God's Word is honorable regardless of our behavior, but Paul seems to be saying there is a direct correlation between the honor the world gives to the Word and the virtue the world sees in Christian women. Think of it! My behavior can determine whether someone else will honor or profane God's Word. That's compelling!

Context of the Command

After planting a church on the Mediterranean island of Crete, Paul left Titus there to organize and instruct the new converts. Titus then faced almost immediate opposition from the enemy of the church; for Satan attempts, not surprisingly, to infect the doctrine, government, and piety of the church. Paul wrote this letter to give Titus authorization and guidance. He instructs Titus in what he should teach and how he should apply it to the various groups within the congregation.

Paul is quite to the point in his description of the situation and the people in Crete:

> For there are many rebellious people, mere talkers and deceivers. . . . They must be silenced, because they are ruining whole households by teaching things they ought not to teach—and that for the sake of dishonest gain. . . . They claim to know God, but by their actions they deny him. They are detestable, disobedient and unfit for doing anything good. (Titus 1:10–11, 16)

Into this context Paul commands Titus to teach the older women so that they can train the younger women to live in such a way that God's Word will not be slandered.

Is there not an alarming parallel between the description of Crete and contemporary America? It is interesting that of all the ways Paul could have told the women to combat the decadence of their culture, he told them to invest their energies in training the younger women to live Christianly in their society. The reputation of the Word of God was at stake. The behavior of Christian women was a pivotal issue, and the involvement of older women was of primary importance. This increases the urgency of the call to today's women: *make an investment in younger women.*

Throughout history the virtue of women has been valued. Scripture teaches: "A wife of noble character who can find? She is worth far more than rubies" (Proverbs 31:10). John Adams, the second president of the United States, said it well:

> From all that I had read of history and government of human life and manners, I had drawn this conclusion, that the manners of women were the most infallible barometer to ascertain the degree of morality and virtue of a nation. The Jews, the Greeks, the Romans, the Swiss, the Dutch, all lost their public spirit and their republican forms of government when they lost the modesty and domestic virtues of their women.[2]

Characteristics of the Command

The specific virtues that Paul tells Titus to teach the older women are not an exhaustive "spiritual maturity" list. These characteristics were extremely relevant to that situation and have no less relevance to our time. Though they may appear

---

It is interesting that of all the ways Paul could have told the women to combat the decadence of their culture, he told them to invest their energies in training the younger women to live Christianly in their society.

---

narrow at first, they are amazingly broad. These particular characteristics were not merely from the mind of Paul; they were divinely inspired by our Sovereign Lord and intended not just for the women in Crete but for His daughters throughout history. These are the virtues that God said would give clarity and distinction to the lives of Christian women living in ungodly surroundings. This places a significance on these four virtues that we are compelled to consider.

Reverent in the way they live. Reverence implies honor, respect, love, and obedience. A reverent life is the product of a reverent view of God. An exalted view of God will shape a Biblical world view that permeates all of life for the woman of faith. A Biblical belief and value system is foundational for a lifestyle of reverence.

Not slanderers. Without control of the tongue, a woman cannot have a positive influence on a younger woman. A critical and complaining spirit is devastating on those who come under its effect. A reverent inner-life will enable a woman to "speak with wisdom, and faithful instruction . . . on her tongue" (Proverbs 31:26).

Not addicted to much wine. Addiction is enslavement. We must be free from habitual, compulsive behavior in order to live disciplined lives for God's glory. Self-control, as opposed to self-indulgence, is the fruit of the Holy Spirit.

Teach what is good. The Greek word translated "good" means beautiful, commendable, excellent. The only legitimate goodness is that which is produced by the Holy Spirit. Teaching what is good is impossible if I don't have the goodness of Christ because my badness will infiltrate my life and my teaching. This goodness is a manifestation of the grace of God within and stands in stark contrast to the standard of goodness that the world contrives.

These virtues, coupled with sound doctrine, give integrity to the ministry older women are to have to younger women. These characteristics indicate spiritual depth and strength. They also imply vulnerability: the older woman must be willing to let a younger woman look into her life and learn from it. She must allow the young woman a close-up view of God's grace in her and His faithfulness to her. This may not be easy. It may be risky. But it imitates the One who allowed us a close-up view of His life so that we could know what God is like: "Anyone who has seen me has seen the Father" (John 14:9).

When a woman embraces these virtues and in the power of the Holy Spirit incorporates them into her life, she has the character and the credibility to encourage and equip a younger woman to live for God's glory.

The Command Itself

This command is in no way intended to be an exhaustive statement about the role of women. The tempo of the letter gives the impression that the gravity of the situation compelled Paul to move immediately to the problem at hand. He tells Titus to teach the older women so that they can train the younger women. This is not the only thing women are to do, but it is an important thing they are to do.

Paul tells Titus to teach the congregation sound doctrine. Then he is to apply that to older women so that they can train the younger women how to live. Why didn't Paul just tell Titus to teach all the people? Truth is truth—isn't it the same for men and women?

I'm sure there are many reasons for Paul's strategy here, but I don't think it takes a rocket scientist to know that men and women are different. God's truth is the same, but our gender sometimes determines how that truth is pushed out into life. No man understands experientially how it feels to be a wife, to have a menstrual cycle, to have a baby, or to go through menopause. Paul was smart enough to know that women need

---

Paul was smart enough to know that women need women to train them how to apply God's Word to areas of our lives that are uniquely feminine.

---

women to train them how to apply God's Word to areas of our lives that are uniquely feminine. In this command, older women are given the high calling of traditioning Biblical womanhood. This is not a ministry of minutia; it is a vital part of church life that must not be pushed to the back-burner.

It would be easy for some women to quickly disqualify themselves by saying, "But I don't have the gift of teaching." Sorry, that won't work! A closer look at the word translated "train" will render that reasoning invalid.

The Greek word is *sophronizo* and denotes "to cause to be of sound mind, to recall to one's senses . . . the training would involve the cultivation of sound judgment and prudence."[3]

This fits with our definition of spiritual mothering:

> When a woman with faith and spiritual maturity enters into a nurturing relationship with a younger woman in order to encourage and equip her to live for God's glory.

The popular concept of mentoring and coaching suggest some degree of structure and formality. Spiritual mothering may involve mentoring and coaching, but it is broader. Nurturing seems to be more compatible with what Paul is advocating in the Titus command.

A nurturing relationship may be structured and ongoing or informal and infrequent. It may be up close or at a distance. It may involve formal instruction, or it may simply mean a weekly telephone call to a new mother who needs support as she adjusts to motherhood. It may mean one-on-one Bible study, or it may mean meeting for lunch once a week to give practical guidance to a colleague about living out her faith in the marketplace. Whatever form it takes, the similarity is that the faith of the younger woman is nourished and enhanced by the relationship.

Whatever the degree of involvement and however the relationship works itself out, the command is clear. Older women are to encourage and equip younger women to live for God's glory. It does not seem to me that this is optional. Titus was not told to teach those women who were interested in signing up for the course. The command seems to be inclusive. The older women in the congregation were to be taught how to live in accordance with sound doctrine so that they could train the younger women—no exceptions.

Who Are the Older Women?

It is impossible from the passage to designate a certain age requirement for older women. Cecil Williamson has explained it this way: "The method used to identify the older women in a local congregation is based on spiritual maturity . . . Those who manifest the Christian virtues given in Titus 2:3 are to be viewed as the mature women in the local congregation."[4]

The character of Christ qualifies a woman to be a spiritual mother. This has nothing to do with biological birthing. It has everything to do with a knowledge of sound doctrine that produces faithful living.

Chronological age is a component because life-experiences provide a valuable resource for training and encouraging younger women. Chronological age gives a view about the life-stage that can only come from living through it. But that still does

---

Whatever the degree of involvement and however the relationship works itself out, the command is clear. Older women are to encourage and equip younger women to live for God's glory.

---

not indicate a specific chronological age. To a degree, we can all be both an older and a younger woman. A spiritually mature woman in her thirties may have a spiritual mother-daughter relationship with a woman in her twenties. The "thirtysomething" woman has lived through the experiences the younger woman is facing and has a perspective that can only come from hindsight. At the same time, the "thirtysomething" woman may be a spiritual daughter to a woman in her fifties while the "twentysomething" woman is "mothering" a teenager struggling to live for God's glory.

The combination of spiritual maturity and life-experiences qualify a woman to nurture a younger woman. Although this combination might be found at any age, my personal observation is that women in their fifties and beyond have a life-perspective that is only possible from living through several life-stages. These women must utilize the lessons learned through their various experiences to encourage and equip younger women to live for God's glory.

Frequently women in their twenties and thirties tell me they want spiritual mothers, but they cannot find older, spiritually mature women who indicate a willingness for such a relationship. Sometimes the situation may be that the older women in the church are new Christians and that younger women are doing the mothering. This role reversal is stretching, but it is workable. My advice to younger women in this situation is to ask the Lord to bring godly older women into their fellowship. In the meantime, they can be mothered "from afar" through books written by Christian women.

To think of yourself as a woman of "sound doctrine" and "spiritual maturity" may seem presumptuous. Perhaps you feel an element of relief because your assessment is that you can honestly disqualify yourself on the basis of these qualifications. Don't sell yourself short, and don't rob the kingdom of what you have to offer! If you are a Christian woman who is seeking to grow in the faith and to live obediently, then you are qualified for spiritual motherhood. If you are not seeking to grow in the faith and to live obediently, then you have a problem that must be confronted! Sound doctrine does not mean that you are a theological expert. Spiritual maturity does not mean that you have reached super sainthood. It does mean that you are growing in your knowledge of the Word and in your desire to apply the Word to every area of your life.

And there are women in your church who need you.

If you rode through Brenda's beautiful neighborhood, you would never guess that inside one of those houses is a woman whose life is in shreds. If you saw Brenda and her family sitting in church each Sunday, you would never guess she is a battered woman. But Eva, an older woman in Brenda's church, did begin to suspect something.

Eva saw Brenda's gradual withdrawal. She doubted Brenda's husband when he told people that Brenda had emotional problems. Her suspicions grew when he insisted that no one from

---

If you are a Christian woman who is seeking to grow in the faith and to live obediently, then you are qualified for spiritual motherhood.

---

the church should visit Brenda. Eva did go to Brenda's home. She read Scripture and prayed with the young woman, and finally Brenda admitted the truth. Eva went with her to talk with the pastor, and eventually the situation was resolved.

Brenda's testimony is that her friends had questioned her, but she would not admit the truth to them. She was too embarrassed to admit that she had come to accept the unacceptable. But something about the love and compassion of an older woman enabled her to break. "As Eva put her arm around me and prayed, I felt like a little girl being loved by her mother, and the tears and words began to flow," she said.

No theological expert. No super saint. Just a woman willing to be obedient to the command to mother.

Celebrating the Command

This command is cause for celebration! Christian women are good at doing what is commanded here. Our femaleness gives us the capacity to nurture and to be nurtured. We bond easily because we have been created with relational strengths. Our faith gives us the Christ-like characteristics to nurture.

This command is also reason for celebration because obedience to it brings out the very best in us. As I write this, we are spending a week at the beach with our children. Watching our daughter Kathryn and her children (Hunter, 24 months, and Mary Kate, 5 months) has reminded me again of the selflessness of mothering. Yesterday our younger daughter Laurin made a beautiful comment: "Being a mother has brought out strength in Kathryn that I never knew she had." It occurred to me that mothering—biological or spiritual—does that. It brings out the best in us because it requires laying self aside.

Evelyn, a regal woman in her late seventies, is one of the many women who has nurtured me during the last three years. I am susceptible to the typical pastor's wife malady: fear of doing anything that will reflect on my husband's ministry and cause trouble for him!

Shortly after moving to our current pastorate, I jokingly made reference to this. Later Evelyn quietly came up to me, put her arm around me, and said, "I can't imagine you doing anything that would upset anyone." Somehow that simple comment liberated me to serve and bonded me to Evelyn. Her vote of confidence gave me the freedom to teach a women's Bible study in our church.

Every time I am around Evelyn, I learn from her and am stimulated by her faith. She has been a widow for seventeen years and has learned that dimension of dependence on God that godly widows possess. One day as I drove by her house, I saw Evelyn on her riding lawnmower. I was struck with how this woman's spiritual strength is matched by her physical strength. Then it occurred to me that God had given her the faith and physical vitality she needs for the task he had assigned her. Evelyn is the caregiver for her retarded brother, Ralph. When I told Evelyn of my "discovery," I immediately realized this was not news to her. Her eyes moistened, and she told me the story.

She was four when her mother died, and her grandmother helped Evelyn's dad raise the children. When Evelyn was thirty-five, her grandmother died. "As she lay dying, she asked me to promise that I would take care of Ralph. I made that promise, and God has enabled me to keep it," she said. Ralph is an institution in our community. He walks to the church every day and carries the mail from the mail box to the church office. He attends every service, and you can often hear him singing the old familiar hymns.

Evelyn's faithfulness to her assigned task has done much more than provide care for her brother. Her steadfast faith and her faithfulness have provided a benchmark for many women. Young women are drawn to her like a magnet. "I want to be like her," they tell me.

"Go for it!" I tell them.

There are wonderful benefits associated with this Titus command. When we make an investment in younger women, we will be enriched personally, the sense of community in the local church will be deepened, society will be blessed, and God's Word will be honored. And that is reason to celebrate!

&a &a &a

A Spiritual Mothering Challenge

1. Begin with prayer.
   a. Meditate on Proverbs 31:30.
   b. Reflect on the virtues listed in the Titus command and ask God to show you the implications of each one for your life.

2. Seek out an older woman who exhibits these virtues and thank her for the example she is to you. Ask her to pray for you and with you as you examine your life in light of these characteristics. My prayer is that you will also have the joyful experience of having a younger woman come to you with this same request.

3. Visit an older woman and ask her these questions:
   - What is a special childhood memory you have?
   - What have you learned about God that you wish you had known when you were twenty-five?

4. If you are a young married woman, visit a widow (or invite her to your home) and ask her to share memories of her husband. Perhaps she even has pictures of her wedding she can show you. Ask her to tell you something she wishes she had known when she first got married.

Barbara's Story

The last sentence in the book of James says, "My brothers, if one of you should wander from the truth and someone should bring him back, remember this: Whoever turns a sinner from the error of his way will save him from death and cover over a multitude of sins" (James 5:19–20). What motivation for discipleship, for spiritual mothering!

This is what Jane did for me. Jane entered my life at a critical time. My spiritual life was a final thin line of smoke rising to the sky. I was dying and miserable inside. I was the wife of a jobless, depressed husband, the mother of a one-year old, and employed by a large company that demanded more of me than I had to give.

I was so unhappy that I cried everyday as I went to work. Then I would sit in my car for ten minutes gathering the strength to enter the building and go through another day. The only thing that brought me home at night was knowing that my daughter was waiting for me.

I knew I needed help, but I honestly didn't know where to go or who to ask. Our pastor had just resigned, and I didn't feel comfortable going to him since he would soon be leaving. Besides, I felt that my misery was something only a woman could understand.

It was during one of those terrible morning drives that I thought of Jane. The fact that I really didn't know her well was part of God's wise plan, for if I had known how busy she was, I never would have asked her for help. But I did muster the courage to ask her if we could talk, and she agreed.

At our first meeting, I shared my circumstances and told her I needed someone to get tough with me, to hold me accountable to what God's Word says, and to prevent me from giving in to my feelings and selfish needs. I needed guidance for practicing the spiritual disciplines. Most of all, I needed someone to pray with me.

God used Jane to turn me from the way of death and to cause a multitude of sins to be covered! As we started meeting regularly to talk, study God's Word, and pray, that spiritual spark started kindling. The icy wall between me and my Creator began to melt. Jane stressed the importance of the discipline of reading God's Word and praying. She had wonderful insights and wisdom for my special needs. Most of all, as my problems grew worse, she did not waver from her stand on Biblical truth. She held fast to God's Word and encouraged me to do the same.

My life isn't perfect, but Jane has taught me to rely upon the Lord. I am grateful that He provided her to stand in the gap and turn me toward Himself.

Recently I thought about all that has gone on in Jane's life during the last year: the death of her mother-in-law, a daughter's deep hurt, being on the committee to find a new pastor for the church, and serving as president of the women's ministry. It suddenly occurred to me that her year had not been easy. Yet she went through the mourning, hurt, discouragement, and fatigue with such grace and trust in God that it seemed effortless. I look forward to the day when, by God's grace, I will be like that.

Barbara Beach
Atlanta, Georgia

4

THE CURRICULUM

*Train the younger women to love their husbands and
children, to be self-controlled and pure, to be busy at home,
to be kind, and to be subject to their husbands.*

Titus 2:4–5

T he topics to be covered in the older-woman/younger
woman "curriculum" are not simply behavioral. They are
expressions of the dominant theme of Paul's letter to Titus. The
theme of godliness is clear from the beginning to the end of the
letter:

> . . . truth that leads to godliness. (1:1)

> For the grace of God that brings salvation has appeared to all
> men. It teaches us to say "No" to ungodliness and worldly
> passions, and to live self-controlled, upright and godly lives
> in this present age. (2:11–12)

> I want you to stress these things, so that those who have
> trusted in God may be careful to devote themselves to doing
> what is good. (3:8)

> Our people must learn to devote themselves to doing what is
> good. (3:14)

Godliness produced by grace gives authenticity to our faith.
Godly living presents a spiritual reality to the world that will
penetrate the darkness of our present age. This reality is to be
evidenced in a life of love that governs women's relationships
and conduct. Thus we might categorize the elements of the curriculum as follows: love, relationships, and conduct.

There seems to be a direct correlation between the characteristics discussed in the last chapter that qualify women to
train younger women, and the elements of the training: reverence (love), not slanderers (relationships), and not addicted
(conduct).

The characteristics are necessary to model the content, and
modeling is probably the most effective way older women train
younger women. At the same time, the church needs to provide
instruction by women for women in these areas. A creative, relevant women's ministry can be the vehicle to teach women
how to deal with the issues they face from a Biblical perspective. Those who lead women's Bible studies should teach Biblical truth and should apply that truth into the practical areas of
a woman's life. I fear that too often the material taught at a
women's Bible study could just as easily be taught by the pastor
for the entire congregation rather than focusing on the specific
needs of and challenges to women. The combination of formal
instruction, in the context of nurturing relationships with older
women who are modeling what is being taught, is the ideal situation.

In this chapter we will give an overview of the broad cate-
gories of the "curriculum." The "how to's" will come later.

Love

> But God demonstrates his own love for us in this: While we
> were still sinners, Christ died for us. (Romans 5:8)

It is appropriate that love is at the top of the list. Though love
is mentioned in the context of teaching women to love their
husbands and children, the underlying principle is that love
must be taught. If we have to be taught how to love our husbands and children, the two most intimate relationships, then
surely we have to be taught simply to love. It is also appropriate
to begin with love because it is love that gives the energy to
work at our relationships and our conduct.

That love must be taught is foreign to much of what we hear and see of love today. Yet the Bible sets forth love as action: "For God so loved that he gave . . ." Biblical love does not

---

Modeling is probably the most effective way older women train younger women.

---

come naturally. Biblical love is produced by the Holy Spirit. We must be taught what this love is and how we are to manifest it in our relationships and conduct.

Paul gives the classic description of Biblical love in 1 Corinthians 13:4–7:

> Love is patient, love is kind. It does not envy, it does not boast, it is not proud. It is not rude, it is not self-seeking, it is not easily angered, it keeps no record of wrongs. Love does not delight in evil but rejoices with the truth. It always protects, always trusts, always hopes, always perseveres.

A reverence for God (the first virtue Paul tells Titus to teach older women) which produces a Biblical view of life is an essential prerequisite for training in love. Love demands dying to self, and this makes no sense until one has come in reverent submission to the authority of God. Love means taking enormous risks, and this surely makes no sense unless one has yielded to the sovereignty of God. So the virtue of reverence is indispensable for both the teacher and the learner in the school of love.

The quality of love should be the identifying mark of the Christian. It is mandatory for our faithful witness.

> A new commandment I give you: Love one another. As I have loved you, so you must love one another. By this all men will know that you are my disciples, if you love one another. (John 13:34–35)

How can we ever forget Francis Schaeffer's comment on these verses?

> If I fail in my love toward Christians, it does not prove that I am not a Christian. What Jesus is saying, however, is that, if I do not have the love I should have toward all other Christians, the world has the right to make the judgment that I am not a Christian.[1]

The pattern for the way we are to love is Jesus Himself. Prior to giving the new commandment in John 13, Jesus gave a powerful object lesson to be sure we understood what love looks like. "Jesus knew that the time had come for him to leave this world and go to the Father. Having loved his own who were in the world, he now showed them the full extent of his love" (John 13:1).

The Master demonstrated the full extent of His love by doing the work of a servant. He "took off his outer clothing, and wrapped a towel around his waist . . . and began to wash his disciples' feet." When He completed the task—to be sure they did not miss the point—He returned to His place at the table, looked directly at them, and said: "Do you understand what I have done for you? . . . I have set you an example that you should do as I have done for you" (John 13:4–5, 12, 15).

Jesus took off the outer clothing that would have hindered his performance of the task. To "do love" we must take off those things that will prevent us from being a servant. This demands dealing with selfishness, pride, laziness, insensitivity, and anything else that hinders our ability to execute love.

It would be an understatement to say that we have our work cut out for us! In our world of me-ism, self-fullfilment, looking out for number one, and all the other dazzling messages women hear, we do not have an easy task. But neither did the women in Crete. We must teach love by demonstrating love. No spoken words will ever teach young women how to love as powerfully as love-filled lives of older women. As young women watch love, day in and day out, they will learn how to do it. And remember, our goal is that younger women be encouraged and equipped to live for God's glory so that His Word will not be maligned.

Relationships

> How great is the love the Father has lavished on us, that we should be called children of God! And that is what we are! (1 John 3:1)

Loving our husbands and children, being kind, and being subject to our husbands—all come under the category of relationships. The second prerequisite for older women—that they are

---

> ### *No spoken words will ever teach young women how to love as powerfully as love-filled lives of older women.*

---

not to be slanderers—seems to fit here. Until a woman has submitted her speech to the Lord, she surely cannot influence a younger woman to build right relationships. Critical words destroy relationships. Younger women need to be taught how to affirm and encourage, how to love and accept, how to influence but not demand.

. . . *to love their husbands and children:* The fact that God has entered into a relationship with us should radically change the way we relate to others. For married women/mothers, the first relationships that should be affected are those within our own families. In our day when the family is at risk, this is surely a relevant topic. Many families are in a danger zone. Christian women teaching younger women how to love their husbands and children can move many of these families into a safety zone.

A wise woman will help a young woman to see the good qualities in her husband and to appreciate him. She will help the young woman to understand the differences between men and women and not to expect her husband to meet all of her needs. She will help a young woman recognize selfish attitudes in herself that are barriers to right relationships in her home. She will help a young woman know how to train her children for righteousness. She will be available to share insights on discipline, standards, and traditions.

At times husbands and children are difficult to love. Often a man who is unemployed or dealing with an illness or facing unusual pressures on the job takes out his frustrations on his wife. A rebellious teenager unleashes enormous anger and frustration on his/her mother. A supportive older woman can "pray through" these times with the younger woman and give her practical advice on loving her husband or child in spite of his/her actions.

Life-experiences and life-observations about family living are rich reservoirs of insights for older women to share with younger women. It is not necessary for all of the older woman's experiences to have been positive. Failures, coupled with the realization of what could have been done differently, are valuable lessons. Just because a woman's teenage or adult children are not walking with the Lord or her marriage has failed does not mean that she is disqualified from encouraging a younger woman in this area.

Widows can be potent encouragers concerning the marriage relationship. After listening to a group of widows share sweet memories of their husbands, one young woman said, "How can I possibly go home and complain about my husband—I just want to go home and love and appreciate him."

Just because a woman is unmarried does not mean she has nothing to offer to younger women regarding family relationships. I know many single women who have incredible insight and wisdom and a unique perspective about children. These women also have a deep understanding of God's Word and a beautiful relationship with the Father. I would listen to their advice any day!

. . . *to be kind:* Kindness is foundational and should characterize our relationships both in and out of the home. The dictionary defines kind as warmhearted, helpful, tolerant, charitable, considerate, thoughtful. Paul gives further definition to kindness when he says, "When the kindness and love of God our Savior appeared, he saved us, not because of righteous things we had done, but because of his mercy" (Titus 3:4–5). God extended kindness to us when we neither deserved nor appreciated it. To emulate our Savior, we are to take kindness to this same level in our relationships—to those who do not "deserve" it and appear not to appreciate it. When a Christian woman extends kindness to the difficult neighbor, the irritable clerk at the supermarket, or the sulking teenager, she carries the warmth of God's love into that relationship.

. . . *to be subject to their husbands:* The topic of submission must be approached with wisdom. We must not handle this topic carelessly. This is a volatile issue that could easily consume an entire book, but here I would simply warn against being extreme in either direction. Unfortunately, Biblical submission has been distorted in both directions. There are those who impose a rigid, almost military-style form of submission that expects a woman to "obey" whatever her husband says. Then there are those who go to the opposite extreme and reject the idea of submission on the grounds of equality.

God's design works. We must not distort that design by going to either extreme. Submission is a clear teaching of Scripture, and older women must help younger women to apply this principle to their marriage relationships. But evangelical women must be very careful that they do not send a false message to women—the message that being "subject to their husbands" means being passive in an abusive situation. Submission does not mean that a woman must suffer abuse or injustice.[2] Our teaching on submission must be carefully developed by thorough study of what God says in His Word. Sound doctrine is essential.

Submission has nothing to do with equality. Men and women are equal, but we have been assigned different roles. Neither role is superior. The Trinity models this concept. The Persons in the Godhead are equal in power and in substance, but each has a different function.

Submission is a position we willingly assume in obedience to Jesus and after His pattern.

> Each of you should look not only to your own interests, but also to the interests of others. Your attitude should be the same as that of Christ Jesus: Who, being in very nature God, did not consider equality with God something to be grasped, but made himself nothing, taking the very nature of a servant. . . . He humbled himself and became obedient to death—even death on a cross! (Philippians 2:4–8)

Submission is an attitude of humility. Submission is being concerned about the interests of another rather than looking after our own interests. The world tells women that submission is foolish and renders us powerless. Scripture tells us that submission gives access to the power and protection of God:

> During the days of Jesus' life on earth, he offered up prayers and petitions with loud cries and tears to the one who could save him from death, and he was heard because of his reverent submission. (Hebrews 5:7)

We must instill in women a vision of enduring relationships and a passion for reflecting Christ in our relationships. We have a generation of young adults who have seen few marriages endure until death parts. With all of our technological advances, it seems we are regressing in the things that really matter—enduring relationships. Older Christian women must communicate a vision of the beauty of a marriage that endures. We must tell young women that the most powerful thing they can do for their children is to love their daddy, for in this way they will show them day in and day out . . . in good times and bad . . . for better or worse . . . what commitment looks like. And we are pathetically short on models of commitment today. Only a passion for God's glory can overpower our self-interest. Submission is simply being empty of self, and this is the key to enduring relationships.

**A disciplined life of purity is
essential to serving our
Father in holiness.**

Older women should also help young women capture the fascinating principle of the Proverbs 31 woman's husband sitting in the gate—i.e., in a place of leadership. When a woman realizes the power of her loving acceptance of her husband and makes an all-out commitment to be his completor and not his competitor, he reaches heights he could never attain without her.

Conduct

Praise be to the Lord, the God of Israel, because he has come and has redeemed his people . . . to enable us to serve him without fear in holiness and righteousness before him all our days. (Luke 1:68, 74–75)

Again it is easy to see the connection between the qualities that are to be taught and the prerequisites for older women. Not addicted to much wine implies self-control, purity, and productivity which have direct bearing on our conduct. A disciplined life of purity is essential to serving our Father in holiness.

Addictions of any kind are a contradiction to self-control, purity, and discipline. With the proliferation of addictions today, we need women who are exercising discipline and who are imposing upon themselves standards of purity in all areas of their lives. Overindulgence in anything eventually enslaves.

Among women, the problems of substance abuse, promiscuity, eating disorders, and soap-opera addictions demand a response. The reasonable response for Christian women is to courageously bring their lives under the authority of God's Word and to live according to His standards of purity. But we must not stop there. We must also lovingly influence other women to this same quality of life—so that God's Word will be venerated.

I do not believe Paul's directive "to be busy at home" sanctions the notion that women are not to be employed outside the home. It would be more logical to put the emphasis on the word *busy*. Considering Paul's description of the people of Crete as "lazy gluttons" (1:12), it seems that Paul is encouraging women to be industrious as opposed to being lazy. This would also be consistent with the description of the virtuous woman in Proverbs 31.

Few would dispute the idea that the best plan is for mothers to remain at home with their children, but for many young women today, that is simply not an option. The virtue of diligence would apply to the homemaker as well as the woman in the marketplace. Older women in both arenas have skills to share that can help younger women. However, in light of what may be a trend among professional women, the opportunities to teach domestic skills may be on the rise. *U.S. News and World Report*, in a June 1991 issue, reported the following:

> Some women are simply ditching the race to the executive suite because the closer they move to the top, the less certain they become that the pinnacle of the men's world is the worthiest of goals. . . . Nearly 30 percent of working women polled last year . . . said that "wanting to put more energy into being a good homemaker and mother" was a reason to consider giving up work indefinitely—an 11 percent increase over 1989 and the highest such figure in 20 years.
>
> Perhaps the sharpest break . . . is a view that true equality can be achieved only if the differences between men and women are valued equally. For some, that means re-emphasizing women's traditional care-giving role in the home; for others, it implies putting a greater focus on integrating "feminine" qualities like nurturing and sharing into the workplace.[3]

Christians should take advantage of this trend and reinforce it. Older Christian women need to remember the "routineness" of homemaking and offer words of support and encouragement. An older woman can pump emotional adrenaline into a young woman by commending her choice to remain at home and by assuring her that her example in the routine of life is shaping the lives of her children.

This return to the home may well provide Christian homemakers with exciting opportunities for friendship evangelism. Where are these women who are leaving the marketplace going to learn domestic skills? Weekly women's Bible studies that offer "special events" such as classes in bread baking, gardening, cooking, and parenting are attracting increasing numbers of women who have left the marketplace and reentered the home. The possibilities are unlimited!

Teaching the Curriculum

Training in love, relationships, and conduct gives substance and significance to spiritual mothering. I can think of no part of life that is not included in one of these elements. When women are encouraging and equipping younger women in these areas of life, they will be teaching what is good, and God will be honored.

My daughter Kathryn is relationship-rich. Even as a little girl, she loved learning from older women. Her first-grade teacher had retired twice but could not stay away from children. Her love for children was only exceeded by her love for her Savior. Clara was in her late sixties when she taught Kathryn. I vividly remember picking Kathryn up from school one day and Clara calling me aside. She was laughing hysterically. "I have to tell you what Kathryn asked me today," she said. "Some of the teenagers came in our room to sell tickets for the high school beauty contest. After they left, Kathryn asked me why I wasn't going to be in the contest."

I assured Clara that the question made perfect sense to Kathryn. In Kathryn's eyes Clara was one of the most beautiful women she had ever seen. Twenty years later, Kathryn still writes to Clara and sends her pictures of her children. Kathryn still remembers lessons this spiritual mother taught her. I think this relationship primed Kathryn's pump. She seems to thrive on learning from older women. I too have learned much from watching her learn!

Just after the birth of Kathryn's second baby, she was paired with an older woman prayer partner in her church. Joanne called Kathryn every week. She simply asked, "How do you need me to pray this week?" Kathryn looked forward to the calls. It was encouraging to know that Joanne was praying. The weeks passed; the relationship grew. One day when Joanne called, Kathryn had real needs. She could confide in Joanne because this woman had spent time cultivating the relationship. Joanne listened, gave wise advice, and practical help. More importantly, she continued to pray.

When Joanne moved to another state, the relationship did not disintegrate. It deepened. Joanne continued to call Kathryn once a week. In order to make the most of those times, she suggested that they select a book to read and discuss. They have worked through several books that have helped Kathryn grow as a young Christian woman. Joanne is patient and gentle with Kathryn, but she "holds her feet to the fire" in encouraging her to press toward spiritual maturity.

How do we teach this curriculum? According to Scripture, the "curriculum" that parents are to teach their children is not found on the pages of a textbook and is not to be taught at 7:00 A.M. The curriculum is a way of life based on Biblical truth. You are to "Impress them on your children. Talk about them when you sit at home and when you walk along the road, when you lie down and when you get up" (Deuteronomy 6:7).

In a similar fashion, the spiritual mothering curriculum is to be impressed on younger women as you prepare the fellowship supper together at church, as you make blankets for the home for unwed mothers, as you sort clothes for the homeless shelter, as you talk about how to maintain a devotional life with three preschoolers competing for your attention, as you walk through the factory making deliveries or into the courtroom to defend a client.

Elisabeth Elliot was only fourteen when she was "introduced" to Amy Carmichael. The headmistress of the school she attended often quoted from Carmichael books. "I was captivated, and told her so. She lent me the books," writes Elisabeth

---

Spiritual mothering has more to do with demonstrating "the shape of godliness" than with teaching lesson plans.

Elliot. "Amy Carmichael became for me what now some call a role model. She was far more than that. She was my first spiritual mother. She showed me the shape of godliness."[4]

Spiritual mothering has more to do with demonstrating "the shape of godliness" than with teaching lesson plans.

Spiritual mothering can happen in individual relationships and in groups. Louise tells how she came out of her "shell of shyness" when she became involved in our weekly women's Bible study. "Sharing and praying in small groups, being paired as prayer partners with older and younger women, laughing and crying together, has been wonderful. As I have learned to open up to other women, I feel like a flower just beginning to open its' petals. I have confidence now to reach out to others. I am experiencing the excitement of being used by my Lord to serve Him."

ع   ع   ع

A Spiritual Mothering Challenge

1. Begin with prayer.
   a. Meditate on Colossians 3:12–17.
   b. These verses from Colossians give guidelines about how we are to relate to one another. Examine your attitudes and actions toward other women in light of these verses. Ask God to shine the light of these verses deep into your heart and to show you anything that is inconsistent with these directions.

2. In the business world, women have "issues breakfasts" when they get together to share information and discuss issues of interest. Why not have an "issues coffee" and invite women to your home for a discussion on "Mothering Teenagers," "Strengthening Your Marriage," "Establishing Meaningful Family Christmas Traditions," "Having a Meaningful Devotional Life," or "How to Love Difficult People." Include women of various ages. You may also want to invite unchurched neighbors.

3. Ask an older or younger woman if she would like to "share a book" with you. Suggest that the two of you read the same book and get together to discuss it.

PART TWO

THE MODEL

At that time Mary got ready and hurried to a town
in the hill country of Judah, where she entered
Zechariah's home and greeted Elizabeth. When
Elizabeth heard Mary's greeting, the baby leaped in
her womb, and Elizabeth was filled with the Holy
Spirit. In a loud voice she exclaimed:
"Blessed are you among women, and blessed is the
child you will bear! But why am I so favored, that
the mother of my Lord should come to me? As soon
as the sound of your greeting reached my ears, the
baby in my womb leaped for joy. Blessed is she who
has believed that what the Lord has said to her
will be accomplished!"
And Mary said: "My soul praises the Lord and my
spirit rejoices in God my Savior, for he has been
mindful of the humble state of his servant. From now
on all generations will call me blessed, for the Mighty
One has done great things for me—holy is his name.
His mercy extends to those who fear him, from
generation to generation. He has performed mighty
deeds with his arm; he has scattered those who are
proud in their inmost thoughts. He has brought down
rulers from their thrones but has lifted up the humble.
He has filled the hungry with good things but has sent
the rich away empty. He has helped his servant
Israel, remembering to be merciful to Abraham and
his descendants forever, even as he said
to our fathers."

Luke 1:39–55

Karen's Story

In 1977 I was going through a very difficult time in my life. Having recently lost a baby late in the pregnancy, and simultaneously gone through the very serious illness of my husband—one that threatened his career, his ministry, and his very life—I was more than ready for some encouragement. In God's good providence, we moved to a small, closely-knit, Bible-believing church where I literally became a sponge, soaking in God's Word as never before.

Although no one in our new church ever made me feel anything but a vital part of the body, as I grew in the knowledge of the Lord, I also grew in the knowledge of how far I had to go. My parents lived thousands of miles away, and I so desperately needed someone to teach me the things I wished my own mother had—how to study God's Word, to be a Christian wife and someday a mother, to be calm, to stay organized, to manage a home, and well, how to be a lady. I wanted a charm school of the spirit, teaching me poise, carriage, and beauty welling up from within my spirit. I didn't want anything to keep God from using me as His vessel.

It wasn't long until I saw a woman who seemed to possess those attributes that I so dearly desired in my own life. I prayed about asking Linda to help me to know what she knew and to do what she did, but I just didn't know how to describe what I wanted her to teach me. One day after church, fumbling for words, I simply blurted out that I wanted her to teach me how to be like her. After initial hesitation, out of modesty and surprise, she must have seen my earnestness. I'll forever love her for her positive response. She invited me to meet with her once a week in her home. The first week, we went over what we wanted to accomplish, beginning from Titus chapter two. Weaving in the disciplines of quiet times, prayer, Scripture memory, and godly submission, we spent part of each "session" in prayer, part in study, and a very large part in questions I had for her. She also recommended a couple of books for me to read, notably *The Disciplines of the Beautiful Woman* by Anne Ortlund.

But Linda wasn't the kind of Titus two woman to merely "schedule" me into her life and then treat me like some "project." She knew that I needed to observe her in action, to follow her example, and to be a part of her life. She and her husband Ted often invited my husband and me for dinner. Her simple, yet nutritious and elegantly-served meals inspired me. I observed as she mothered her two girls and met her husband at the end of the day. I was completely unaware of just how much of all this was engineered for my benefit. At the time, it seemed as if we were just building a friendship—and we were—but looking back, I can see the footprints of her careful attention.

We actually only met together on a regular basis for a couple of months. But as time passed, Linda would periodically invite me to participate in an evangelistic coffee she was hosting in her home or a neighborhood Bible study, or just drop by for a visit and a cup of tea. How my eyes followed her every move, from the way she greeted her guests, arranged her furniture, and unpacked her groceries, to her fervent prayers for lost souls.

Now separated by many miles and many years, I still remember Linda gratefully and in awe. Because somehow, in my youthful desire to be like her, she guided me in discovering how to be like Him.

Karen Grant
Franklin, Tennessee

5

A NURTURING
RELATIONSHIP

Mary . . . hurried to a town in the hill country of Judah,
where she entered Zechariah's home and greeted Elizabeth.

Luke 1:39

L et's examine once again our definition of spiritual
mothering:

> When a woman of faith and spiritual maturity enters into a
> nurturing relationship with a younger woman in order to en-
> courage and equip her to live for God's glory.

Mary and Elizabeth illustrate our spiritual mothering definition and serve as a commentary on the Titus mandate. We do
not know Mary's emotional condition when she reached
Elizabeth's door, but we do know that only moments in
Elizabeth's presence produced Mary's Magnificat that has
brought glory to God and blessing to his people for centuries.
Mary was encouraged and equipped to glorify God. By examin-
ing what happened between these women, we can see that the
definition of spiritual mothering begins with the establishment
of a relationship.

Spiritual mothering is impossible apart from a relationship.
But just any relationship will not do. Our definition goes on to
qualify the kind of relationship that is necessary. It must be a
nurturing relationship. Nurturing relationships do not just happen. They require work and wisdom. A close look at the Mary-

Elizabeth model will give us some principles that will help us establish nurturing relationships.

Grace: The Connector of the Relationship

The angel told Mary that her relative Elizabeth was also expecting a child. This news validated his next statement: "For nothing is impossible with God" (Luke 1:37). Elizabeth's biological clock had wound down. She had never conceived, and now it was humanly impossible. But God put life in her dead womb just as He put life in Mary's virgin womb. Both of these women experienced the life-giving power of God; both were recipients of His grace. There was a blood connection between them, but it did not begin to compare with this grace-connection.

Every Christian has also experienced this same life-giving power of God:

> As for you, you were dead in your transgressions and sins, . . .
> But because of his great love for us, God, who is rich in mercy, made us alive with Christ. . . . (Ephesians 2:1, 4)

Any two women who have had the glorious experience of receiving spiritual life are in relationship with one another because they are in relationship with Jesus. God establishes the relationship; we must cultivate and celebrate it. Mary and Elizabeth did this—Mary went to Elizabeth, and they celebrated God's grace as they worshipped Him through praise. Worship is the first and foremost way we celebrate God's grace. Since only believers can worship in spirit and in truth, worship is one of the most intimate ways we celebrate God's grace together. When two women join together in the study of God's Word, prayer, and praise, they enjoy an eternal bond that is possible only because of God's grace.

The beauty of this principle is that when grace is the connector between women, they are able to enter into a mutually nurturing relationship that enriches them both. But the pain of the principle is that many women have a biological mother or daughter who has not experienced God's saving grace. There is then a dimension to the relationship that is simply impossible. This is very painful for the woman who longs to have that di-

---

When two women join together in the study of God's Word, prayer, and praise, they enjoy an eternal bond that is possible only because of God's grace.

---

mension with the mother or daughter she loves so dearly. However, the believer must be careful not to let her hurt become disappointment in the unbeliever, which will quickly degenerate to resentment. She must constantly remember that her own salvation is purely of grace and that she in no way deserves it. She must pray for and love the unbeliever. She must pray for patience to understand that the unbeliever's limitations are the limitations of spiritual deadness and that only God can create spiritual life. This gives great hope because He is a God of grace.

A Nurturing Relationship Must Be Cultivated

I think Mary and Elizabeth could celebrate because a relationship was already in place. God did not choose two strangers. It seems that Mary had some degree of confidence in that relationship to go to Elizabeth with this incredible story.

I wonder what kind of cultivating Elizabeth had done. Perhaps she had visited in Mary's home and always took time to talk with Mary. Perhaps she wrote Mary notes of encouragement. Perhaps she praised qualities of excellence in Mary's character that no one else noticed. Whatever she did, it seems that Elizabeth's home was a safe place for Mary. But it is significant that Mary went to Elizabeth—the younger woman went to the older woman.

A spiritual mother is willing to cultivate a relationship with a younger woman by spending time with her on what may seem trivial matters: teaching her to bake bread, meeting for breakfast to discuss a situation at work, keeping her children so she can have a night out with her husband, taking her to lunch. This opens the way for the younger woman to share her story with the older woman. But younger women need to follow Mary's example and seek out older women who display evidence of God's grace and ask for their help to live for God's glory. Often older women are willing, but they feel it would be presumptuous to approach a younger woman. Older women can do the cultivating, but younger women need to do the instigating.

Age Differences Enrich a Relationship

These women were from two different generations, yet the generation gap was bridged by God's grace. God purposely chose an older woman and a younger woman for two unique missions: for the one, being the mother of the Messiah's forerunner, for the other, being the mother of the Messiah. He made each of the women aware of the assignment He had given to the other; apparently He wanted Mary to have the support and encouragement of an older woman. This is, of course, consistent with the command He gives us in Titus.

This makes me wonder about Mary's biological mother. Could she not have supplied the nurturing by an older woman that Mary needed? Scripture tells us nothing about Mary's mother, but I can think of at least three possibilities.

- She was not alive.
- She was alive but did not believe Mary's story.
- She was alive, she believed and supported Mary, and she encouraged her to visit Elizabeth because she wanted her

daughter to have the wisdom and nurturing of other women besides herself.

I like the third possibility. This is as it should be. Mothers of adult daughters should encourage them to cultivate relationships with as many older women as possible. No matter how solid our relationships are with our biological daughters, their lives will be richer if they are also nurtured by other women. I do believe that biological mothers can and should be spiritual mothers to their daughters, but our biological connection sometimes blurs our vision. I know—I have two adult daughters.

As my daughters were becoming adults, I tried hard to redefine our relationships and to move into the spiritual mothering role. We talk a lot about this, and most of the time, we do quite well. I can usually be objective and can encourage them to act Biblically even in difficult circumstances. But there are

> **No matter how solid our relationships are with our biological daughters, their lives will be richer if they are also nurtured by other women.**

times when I have myopic vision regarding my girls. This happened recently when my oldest daughter, Kathryn, had been hurt in a relationship. Instead of encouraging humility, gentleness, and forgiveness, I have to admit that I over-looked her self-centeredness and agreed that she had been treated unfairly. Later that day, Joanne, Kathryn's older-woman-prayer-partner from church, called. This very wise woman encouraged Kathryn to exhibit the Christ-like virtues that were needed in the situation. That night I was convicted about my failure to encourage obedience regardless of circumstances. The next morning I called Kathryn to tell her I blew it and ask for her forgiveness.

She told me about her conversation with Joanne, and I praised God for another older woman in my daughter's life who did not have the blind spots that I often have.

I must add that Kathryn was very understanding of my limitations. Her comment was, "Mom, when Hunter is playing with a little friend and I see him grab a toy from his friend's hand, I know it is wrong. But something inside me wants to let Hunter have whatever he wants. I don't want to make him give it back. I understand how hard it is for you to always look at things objectively. Sometimes mother-love just gets in the way." She is so right. Perhaps Mary's mother knew this and realized her daughter needed the objective love of an older woman who could encourage and equip her for the task she had been given.

A Nurturing Relationship Serves

A nurturer is concerned about the growth and development of the one being nurtured. In our context, the nurturer is promoting spiritual growth and development; therefore, this is not a self-centered, self-serving relationship. Nurturing involves serving, which drives us again to grace. Because of our sin nature, we are incapable of living anything other than a self-centered life apart from grace.

Elizabeth entered into a nurturing relationship because by grace she had defined herself as a servant. When she saw Mary, Elizabeth said, "Why am I so favored, that the mother of my Lord should come to me?" The Greek word translated "Lord" is *kurios,* which means master, owner. Here Elizabeth acknowledged God as the Master and Owner of her life. We have already seen that Mary's response to the angel's announcement was, "I am the Lord's servant." This implies certain characteristics of a nurturing relationship. I think these characteristics come into sharp focus when we consider some of the ways God says we are to relate to one another:

Be completely humble and gentle; be patient, bearing with one another in love. Make every effort to keep the unity of the Spirit through the bond of peace. (Ephesians 4:2–3)

Do nothing out of selfish ambition or vain conceit, but in humility consider others better than yourselves. Each of you should look not only to your own interests, but also to the interests of others. Your attitude should be the same as that of Christ Jesus: Who, being in very nature God, did not consider equality with God something to be grasped, but made himself nothing, taking the very nature of a servant. . . . (Philippians 2:3–7)

Therefore, as God's chosen people, holy and dearly loved, clothe yourselves with compassion, kindness, humility, gentleness and patience. Bear with each other and forgive whatever grievances you may have against one another. Forgive as the Lord forgave you. And over all these virtues put on love, which binds them all together in perfect unity. (Colossians 3:12–14)

This way of relating is diametrically opposed to how the world tells us to relate. This outworking of God's grace in us is demonstrated in relationships.

This is the right thing to do and the pleasant thing to do: "How good and pleasant it is when brothers [and sisters] live together in unity!" (Psalm 133:1).

But it is not always the easy thing to do! Again the answer is grace—God's grace that liberates us to be a servant. The classic Biblical passage on servanthood gives marvelous clues about the knowledge that is necessary to be a servant/nurturer.

It was just before the Passover Feast. Jesus knew that the time had come for him to leave this world and go to the Father. Having loved his own who were in the world, he now showed them the full extent of his love.

The evening meal was being served. . . . Jesus knew that the Father had put all things under his power, and that he had come from God and was returning to God; so he got up from the meal, took off his outer clothing, and wrapped a towel around his waist. After that, he poured water into a

basin and began to wash his disciples' feet, drying them with
the towel that was wrapped around him. . . .

When he had finished washing their feet, he put on his
clothes and returned to his place. "Do you understand what I
have done for you?" he asked them. . . . "I have set you an
example that you should do as I have done for you." (John
13:1–5, 12, 15)

A woman who struggles with poor self-image is so enslaved
that she cannot be a servant/nurturer. The only adequate anti-
dote for the self-image problem is a Biblical knowledge of ourselves. In this passage we see that Jesus knew four things about
Himself:

- He knew that "the time" had come.
- He knew the outcome—"the Father had put all things
  under His power."
- He knew from where He had come.
- He knew to where He was going.

"So, he . . . took off his outer clothing . . . and began to
wash his disciples' feet." Based upon this knowledge of Himself
He took off those things that hindered Him and served His disciples. And He tells us to do the same thing. The glorious truth
is that we can have this same knowledge about ourselves which
will free us from the things that hinder us from being ser-
vant/nurturers.

We know that our time has come:

From one man he made every nation of men, that they
should inhabit the whole earth; and he determined the times
set for them and the exact places where they should live.
(Acts 17:26)

Amazing! Our sovereign God planned the exact time in
history and the exact place on this planet that we would live.
He designed the exact set of circumstances through which we
are living at any given moment. This is the place, the time, and
the situation that God wants me to use for His glory. This is so

exciting and so liberating! Seeing life from this faith perspective removes the hindrances of self-pity and boredom.

We know the outcome:

> And we know that in all things God works for the good of those who love him, who have been called according to his purpose. For those God foreknew he also predestined to be conformed to the likeness of his Son. (Romans 8:28–29)

Since all things are "under his power," He can and will determine the outcome. We may not understand *how* God is going to work out the things in our lives for good, but we know that He is going to do it. He will use everything to conform us

---

The only adequate antidote for the self-image problem is a Biblical knowledge of ourselves.

---

to the likeness of Jesus—and that is the ultimate good! This knowledge frees us from the hindrance of fear.

We know where we came from:

> For he chose us in him before the creation of the world to be holy and blameless in his sight. In love he predestined us to be adopted as his sons through Jesus Christ, in accordance with his pleasure and will. . . . (Ephesians 1:4–5)

Talk about roots! We have family roots that go back to eternity past. We belong to God's family! This knowledge gives a sense of identity and belonging. It removes the hindrances of insecurity and loneliness.

We know where we are going:

> Do not let your hearts be troubled. Trust in God; trust also in me. In my Father's house are many rooms; if it were not so, I would have told you. I am going there to prepare a place for you. And if I go and prepare a place for you, I will come back and take you to be with me. (John 14:1–3)

The knowledge of our eternal destiny gives a calmness and confidence regardless of present circumstances. My friend, Dot, has a wonderful perspective. Whenever things are difficult, she says, "In the light of eternity, what does it really matter?" This eternal perspective brings things into focus. It removes the hindrances of frustration and fretting about circumstances.

This Biblical knowledge of ourselves enables us to lay aside all that restricts us from entering into nurturing relationships with others. This Biblical self-view is what older women need to possess and to share with younger women.

It takes time and effort, but such a nurturing relationship will bring forth praises to God.

❧   ❧   ❧

A Spiritual Mothering Challenge

1. Begin with prayer.
   a. Reflect again on the John 13 passage. What is hindering you from being a servant/nurturer? Consider each of the four things we can know about ourselves and "take off" those hindrances in light of this Biblical self-knowledge.
   b. Is there a close relative in your life who is not a Christian? The limitations in your relationship are painful, but they must not cause you to be resentful. Ask God for grace to accept and love her.

2. Evaluate your relationships. Are you a servant/nurturer? Do you have relationships with women of different ages? If so, get together and celebrate them. If not, what can you do to cultivate them?

3. If there is a college in your community, contact them about inviting international women to your home. International students long for opportunities to be in American homes. Establishing nurturing relationships with these young women can provide incredible opportunities to demonstrate the love of Jesus.

Leslie's Story

I consider myself to be immensely privileged to have been placed by God in Naples, Florida, at Covenant Presbyterian Church in the early 1980s. Most of the women involved in the church at that time were older women in their retirement years. These active, deeply committed Christian women saw their age as a blessing and not a hindrance. Their desire to see others grow in the Lord translated into spiritual blessings for me.

My husband sensed the call to pastoral ministry in 1981. We both wanted to avoid making a rushed decision so we spent the next two years "preparing to be prepared." During this time many women made significant investments in my preparation.

A couple who had been on the mission field for more than forty years became surrogate grandparents to our children. She told me marvelous stories of God's faithfulness in their lives. Because her love for the Lord was so obvious and her trust in Him so deep, I listened intently. She built into me a desire to trust and obey my Savior. She also made me laugh so much that I couldn't wait to be with her!

Our pastor's wife was another source of great love. She let me into her home and her heart. She asked me to help her lead a Bible study. I couldn't believe she would trust me with that responsibility, and I was eager to live up to that trust.

Another woman helped me understand that God loved me. We had many long telephone conversations. I'll never forget her words: "You are a child of the King; you must learn to live like a princess!" A Scripture verse she framed for me still hangs on our wall to remind me that when God has tested me, I "will come forth as gold."

Thinking of how these women influenced me is like playing back a file of tapes that flood my memory. There are fast moving pictures of bags of groceries at our door, a $20 bill in an envelope every week for six weeks when my husband's job was eliminated, invitations to dinner, and going home with the leftovers! There are slow moving pictures of words spoken, prayers prayed, and loving hugs that encouraged.

When we left to enter Bible college, my greatest fear was being without the security and friendship these women gave me. But I soon understood that this separation was God's way of helping me to begin to fulfill my desire to be like those women.

Throughout our four years in college and four more years in seminary, those dear women never forgot us. There were letters, assurances of prayer, checks, boxes of clothing—and more boxes of clothing as our family increased to four children!

During our seminary years, I worked with seminary wives in support groups and activities as we prepared for life in ministry. I shared with them what the women in our home church did for us. Thus, the influence of those faithful women rippled out far beyond my own family. Their example taught many of us how women can minister to other women.

We will graduate soon. We don't know yet where God will lead us. But I do know this. My heart's desire is to be to other women what the women in my local church have been to me.

Leslie Singenstreu
St. Louis, Missouri

6

ENCOURAGE AND EQUIP

In a loud voice she exclaimed:
"Blessed are you among women . . . !"

Luke 1:42

S ix brief verses describe the meeting between Elizabeth and Mary that led to Mary's song of praise. But those verses contain volumes about how older women can encourage and equip younger women to live for God's glory.

As Mary traveled from Nazareth to the hill country of Judah, perhaps she wondered how Elizabeth would react to her story. Would she believe her or would she reject her? *Be real, Mary—an angel? You're pregnant and still a virgin?* But Mary was not kept guessing about Elizabeth's reaction.

> In a loud voice she [Elizabeth] exclaimed: "Blessed are you among women, and blessed is the child you will bear! But why am I so favored, that the mother of my Lord should come to me? As soon as the sound of your greeting reached my ears, the baby in my womb leaped for joy. Blessed is she who has believed that what the Lord has said to her will be accomplished!" (Luke 1:42–45)

Elizabeth's verbal affirmation poured encouraging energy into Mary that caused her to praise God and to rejoice in Him. This is what older women who want to obey the Titus command must do for younger women.

Verbal Affirmation

Verbal affirmation is essential to encouraging and equipping because women need the approval of other women. Simply with-
holding criticism is not sufficient. We must express approval. I
have heard women say, "I just can't do that. I didn't grow up
being open and verbal, and it isn't natural for me." That is no
excuse. You may have to unlearn and relearn, and it may be
difficult. But it is not impossible, and to be a spiritual mother, it
is essential. We should not leave women guessing like my friend
who said, "I think my mother is proud of me because her friends
frequently tell me positive things she said about me—but she
has never said any of those things to me, so I'm not sure."

I am often reminded of the importance of verbal affirmation
when I am with my married daughter and I say something such
as, "Kathryn, you are a terrific wife," or "You are a wonderful
mother." Almost always her response is, "Do you really think
so?" I have told her so hundreds of times, but she needs to hear
me say it hundreds more times. Being a good wife and mother
are of great importance to her, and she needs to know that her
mother approves of how she is doing.

But verbal affirmation alone is not what we are talking
about. Words that encourage and equip a woman to live for
God's glory are much more than flattery. Before we read
Elizabeth's words of encouragement, we read that "Elizabeth was
filled with the Holy Spirit." These were Spirit-led words with a
purpose—God's glory. This makes Elizabeth's words worth ex-
amining.

"*Blessed are you among women . . .*" (*v. 42*). The word
translated "blessed" means "to speak well of, praise."[1] Surely
Mary must have had some concern about her reputation. Who
would believe that she had not lost her virginity before marriage? How would she handle the gossip in Nazareth? Elizabeth
immediately assures her that women will speak well of her and
praise her. She was so convincing that Mary responded, "From
now on all generations will call me blessed."

The teenager who confides in you that she is pregnant does not need to be convinced that she did wrong. She needs to hear that you will support her and that other women will be grateful if she makes a pro-life choice and does not abort the baby. The woman who tells you she had an abortion as a teenager and that she has lived with guilt since becoming a Christian does not need condemnation. She needs to know that God can use it for good—perhaps she will be used to begin a post-abortion ministry to other women. Words that hold out hope that God will use the situation in a positive way are energizing.

"*. . . and blessed is the child you will bear!*" (*v. 42*). Had Mary worried about the names her Child might be called by those who thought she conceived before marriage? Again Elizabeth assures her that people of faith will "speak well of and praise" this Child.

When one of our children went through a time of rebellion, I knew the pain of other women's criticism. I also knew the comfort of women who gave me hope and encouragement. My friend Sue's words still ring loudly in my ears: "In God's economy nothing is wasted. He will redeem this time and use it for good." She did not just tell me that once; over and over she assured me. She never made me think that I had failed as a mother. Her words bonded me to her. And when that "prodigal" did return, Sue was a part of the celebration. She has continued to celebrate with me as we have watched God use the things learned during that rebellious time and as we have rejoiced in the spiritual growth of that child.

Approachable Spirit

"*But why am I so favored that the mother of my Lord should come to me?*" (*v. 43*). Elizabeth was so approachable! She wanted to be sure that Mary felt welcome. She unselfishly laid aside the excitement about her own pregnancy. "Mary, you could have chosen any woman—thank you for choosing to share your wonderful news with me."

I don't go to some women because they give the impression that they are too distracted by things in their own lives to hear me. I don't go to others because I am never sure about their moods. Sometimes I feel a warmth and openness but just as often I feel as if I am standing before a stone wall. I usually won't take the risk of going to these women. But I do go to those who make it easy for me. I do go to those who tell me by their attitude and words that they are glad I have come.

Challenge to Be Obedient

"Blessed is she who has believed that what the Lord has said to her will be accomplished" (v. 45). Elizabeth affirmed Mary's faith and challenged her to continue to believe God's Word. The word translated "blessed" here means happy, fortunate. Elizabeth reminded Mary that it is obedience to the Word of God that brings true happiness. She must pursue holiness, not happiness. The pursuit of happiness leads to emptiness, but in God's economy, the pursuit of holiness leads to real and lasting happiness. When obedience is affirmed it usually produces more obedience.

Older women must be saturated with God's Word and hold it before young women as the standard for faith and practice. Every belief and every action must line up with God's truth if it is going to encourage and equip younger women to live for His glory.

> All Scripture is God-breathed and is useful for teaching, rebuking, correcting and training in righteousness, so that the man of God may be thoroughly equipped for every good work. (2 Timothy 3:16)

> The law of the LORD is perfect, reviving the soul. The statutes of the LORD are trustworthy, making wise the simple. The precepts of the LORD are right, giving joy to the heart. The commands of the LORD are radiant, giving light to the eyes. The fear of the LORD is pure, enduring forever. The

ordinances of the LORD are sure and altogether righteous. They are more precious than gold, than much pure gold; they are sweeter than honey, than honey from the comb. By them is your servant warned; in keeping them there is great reward. (Psalm 19:7–11)

Brevity of Expression

The brevity of Elizabeth's remarks is to be commended. Women's verbal strengths often cause us to be excessive in our expressions. Some women say so many words that it is difficult to filter out the real message. That was no problem for Mary because Elizabeth "cut to the chase" and succinctly said what needed to be said.

Several years ago I was dealing with a situation and shared it with Frances, an older friend. I really don't even remember what the situation was, but I clearly remember her listening intently and then saying, "Susan Hunt will do the right thing." Frances believed in me; she had confidence that I would act obediently in that situation. There was no way I would waver after that affirmation. Her words have remained with me long after my memory of the situation. Many times when I have been faced with the choice of obedience, those brief seven words have stabilized my thinking.

Mary stayed with Elizabeth three months. I feel sure that Elizabeth continued to encourage and equip the young woman. There were probably practical discussions about being a wife and mother. Perhaps there were cooking lessons and advice about budgeting time and money. But Elizabeth began with verbal affirmation that surely was like the balm of Gilead to young Mary.

The woman of noble character who is worth more than rubies "speaks with wisdom, and faithful instruction is on her tongue" (Proverbs 31: 26).

Joseph "Skip" Ryan has written some very practical advice about our speaking:

Paul says, "Be filled with the Spirit, speaking to one another in psalms, hymns . . ." (Ephesians 5:18). He is concerned here about the conversations that lead to spiritual encouragement and ultimately to worship. Real spirituality often is revealed by the way we communicate with our friends. So the right questions are: Do our friendships lead us to the Lord in praise? And how do we foster spiritual friendship by the way we speak?

First, our speaking should reveal that we are submitting to one another. Being filled with the Spirit (Ephesians 5:18) results in being subject to one another (Ephesians 5:21). Submission demonstrates the Spirit's presence in a friendship. Our ministry is not to be programs but rather the laying down of our lives. . . . Does my speaking reveal my self-importance or a more realistic humility?

Second, our speaking should demonstrate that we prize diversity. We must resist making everyone look and act just like us. We learn the most in our ministries from those who are different from us. We affirm diversity (with words) because it is a truer picture of the church as a body. We affirm others' callings and gifts (with words) because collegiality is a more Biblical way to minister.

Third, our speaking should solve the problems of diversity. Diversity causes problems. The solution: Keep short accounts; don't accumulate a list and dump. Agree to be open about competition and jealousy. We pretend these things don't exist, but they are in the soil of our hearts and ministries, and they hinder what grows there.

Finally, our speaking should create an atmosphere of fun. Some have left the ministry because of a wooden and sullen atmosphere without laughter. One such friend, now in business, told me, "I have friends now, real friends, go-get-pizza-together friends." The language of laughter should characterize our friendships. . . .

The way we speak speaks loudly about our own spirituality and our friendships. "Then those who feared the Lord talked with each other." (Malachi 3:16)[2]

Elizabeth opened her door and her heart to Mary. She also opened her mouth and spoke words of affirmation. Mary's re-

> **We must not allow the voices of the world to set the agenda for this decade, nor must we allow those voices to teach women how to be women.**

sponse to Elizabeth's words is truly magnificent because it magnifies the grace and mercy of God. The '90s woman has grown up in a culture that magnifies "personal peace and affluence" as Francis Schaeffer said. This generation of women has never known a time when they could not legally get an abortion because "they have a right" to their own bodies. They grew up on a self-centered approach to life, and many of them have had no role models of Christian values.

Who is assuming responsibility to transmit Biblical values to these women? What world and life view is being communicated to women today? We hear that this is the decade of women. We must not allow the voices of the world to set the agenda for this decade, nor must we allow those voices to teach women how to be women. Christian women must speak with boldness and clarity about womanhood and must live distinctly Christian lives. Christian women must articulate a Biblical world and life view and the implications of this perspective for women.

Women are spiritual trend-setters. Today many women are buying into New Age philosophies because they are looking for hope in their hopelessness. We must not abandon these women. We must come alongside and encourage and equip them to live for God's glory. When we reach women, we will reach the spiritual tempo of our culture. This is a doable task, as one by one we become Elizabeths for that woman on our doorstep. But we cannot do it by remaining silent. We must speak the words of life:

> Gold there is, and rubies in abundance, but lips that speak knowledge are a rare jewel. (Proverbs 20:15)

&a.   &a.   &a.

A Spiritual Mothering Challenge

1. Begin with prayer.

   a. Reflect on Proverbs 10:11.

   b. Are your words a fountain of life? How often do you verbally affirm other women? How often do you say, "I love you . . . I appreciate you . . . I am proud of you"?

   c. Prayerfully make a list of women God lays on your heart. Write beside each name something that you admire or appreciate about her. Within the next week speak those words to those women. Make this a weekly practice, and there will be scores of women who will be encouraged and equipped to live for God's glory.

2. Write a young woman away in college and tell here you are praying for her. You can really make her day by sending a "goodie box."

Diane's Story

The "older woman" who made a deep impression on me was eighteen. I was seventeen. I wasn't a Christian, but on Sundays I acted the part and went to church with my mother. Patty approached me one Sunday. She was pretty and outgoing, and I was flattered that she would talk with me. "Your mom said you may be interested in coming to our youth Bible study on Wednesdays," she said. "That sounds great," I lied. I had no intention of going to church twice in one week.

By Wednesday I had forgotten the conversation, but Patty remembered. When I answered the telephone, her bright voice on the other end of the line said, "We're all here. Where are you?" I reluctantly drove to the house where they were meeting. Patty was waiting and warmly welcomed me.

What I encountered when I entered that group was something I had never experienced. Teen-age girls were worshipping the Lord. The predominant atmosphere was one of praise to God. These girls were my age, yet they talked to God as though He was in that very room. I was captivated. As I sat among them, I was overwhelmed with an intense desire to have that kind of relationship with God.

Patty sat beside me as I discovered Christ as my personal Savior. After I prayed, Patty opened a large spiral notebook and explained to me how a person grows through daily Bible reading and prayer. I was moved by her concern for me. But I was even more moved by her love for Jesus.

Patty persevered. The next day she called to see if I had any doubts or questions. I did, so she invited me to spend the night at her home. I expected a family of "spiritual giants," so you can imagine my surprise to learn that Patty was the only Christian in her home. We spent hours in her room talking, praying, and praising God.

The years have passed. My husband and I have spent over twenty years on the mission field. I lost contact with Patty, but I have not forgotten her. I always prayed that some day I would have the opportunity to influence teen-age girls the way Patty influenced me. When we were serving in Mexico, the Lord answered that prayer and gave me the opportunity to work with a group of seven young debutantes. These girls were new in Christ and hungry for growth, but they were struggling with the decisions and changes that life brings to young women. I realized that the Lord had put me in their lives at a pivotal point. Watching the spiritual growth of these young women was like watching petals on a flower unfold. I often wonder if Patty had this experience as she watched my growth.

My husband and I have served in many parts of the world. Many times I think of Patty and wish I could tell her what an encouragement she was to me. Her faithfulness at eighteen still challenges me today.

Dianne Smalling
Missionary in Ecuador

7

TO LIVE
FOR GOD'S GLORY

*My soul praises the Lord, and
my spirit rejoices in God my Savior.*

Luke 1:46

Focusing on God's glory gives beauty and depth to the spiritual mother-daughter relationship. The mutual desire to live for God's glory makes the relationship work. There are basically two approaches to life: self-centered or God-centered. Since both Mary and Elizabeth had embraced God's glory as the intensity of their lives, they shared a common purpose. This freed them from a self-centered approach to life and relationships. It doesn't mean that they ceased to struggle with self-centeredness. Surely these women were not immune to the internal sin-struggles that plague us all. They were not oblivious to self-centeredness, but they were obedient to God's Word.

What difference does it make in our relationships when we share the life-purpose of glorifying God? There is, of course, an inexhaustible list. But as we examine what this looked like in our Mary-Elizabeth model, we can see some essential differences that distinguish a spiritual mother-daughter relationship.

Biblical World View
Replaces "My" World View

The extent of a newborn's world is himself/herself. The circle of the infant's concern is what makes him/her feel good. The infants cry signals the others in his/her life to come change, feed, burp, or hold—*now*. The sad truth is that for many people their world view circle never gets much larger. Their socialization experiences may help them handle it with a little more sophistication, but basically their world view is "what works for me." This pitifully shallow approach to life leads to emptiness and despair. The cry of this infant world view is "Come into my world and make me happy"—a definite deterrent to healthy relationships.

When a person is saved by God's grace and begins to understand the magnitude of His sovereignty, the "my" world view is replaced by a Biblical world view. Growth in the grace and knowledge of God pushes the circle out to encompass His sovereign plan for His world. We see ourselves, our circumstances, and our relationships as a part of His divine plan. So our approach changes from "Come into my world and make me happy," to "Father, show me how to go into Your world and glorify You." The effect on a relationship is a switch from wanting you to serve me to a desire to serve God through the relationship.

Mary and Elizabeth demonstrate a Biblical world view.

When Mary was confronted with the announcement that she would give birth to the Messiah, think of what she did *not* say:

- "You'll have to give me time to process this, and I'll get back with you. I'm not sure this would meet my needs right now."
- "But Joseph and I are planning a big wedding—I don't know if I can handle the disappointment!"
- "I'm just not ready to be a mother. I need my space. Anyway, Joseph and I were planning to be a two-career couple so that we can buy a house before we start a family. I don't think this would work for us."

> *Our approach changes from "Come into my world and make me happy," to "Father, show me how to go into Your world and glorify You."*

Mary's immediate and unequivocal response was: "I am the Lord's servant." Mary was aware that something much bigger than her personal agenda was going on here. Suddenly she was catapulted to center-stage in world history.

Elizabeth, too, was apparently aware that she was a part of God's plan. Elizabeth and her husband were "upright in the sight of God, observing all the Lord's commandments and regulations blamelessly" (Luke 1:6). Elizabeth had no children and was past child-bearing age. Yet she continued to live obediently. The fact that she observed *all* the Lord's commandments blamelessly tells me something about the world view of this woman. Though her heart must have been saddened by her barrenness, she did not become barren in her spirit. She did not allow self-pity and depression to immobilize her and to reduce her circle of concern. She lived obediently in spite of her circumstances. When God worked the miracle of life in her womb, her response was, "The Lord has done this for me" (Luke 1:25). She was under no illusions about the Source of this life within her.

It seems obvious to me that these women understood that they were part of God's plan. Their world and life view was much bigger than their own worlds because God's glory was their life-purpose. They could accept and adjust to the changes that came into their lives because they were centered on God and not self. This affected their relationship because they were not in two different circles. Mary was not in her circle calling for Elizabeth to come "fix" it, and Elizabeth was not in her circle expecting Mary to come in and meet her needs. They were already in the same circle—God's circle.

Humility Replaces Pride

Humility is a hallmark of the Christian life. Humility replaces pride when we are stripped of self and glorifying God becomes the compelling force in our lives. Humility is not a passive, syrupy sweetness. Humility is rugged obedience. And this dramatically affects the way we relate to one another.

I am impressed that Mary went to Elizabeth. Pride could have caused her to say, "If Elizabeth wants to see the mother of the Messiah, let her come to Nazareth. Why should I make that difficult trip?" Mary was teachable. A teachable spirit is evidence of humility.

Elizabeth's humility is evidenced in her remark to Mary, "But why am I so favored, that the mother of my Lord should come to me?" Pride did not cause her to think, "Why did Mary get the greater honor. I am the oldest. I have lived obediently all these years, and what did it get me—second place! And I taught that young thing everything she knows!"

They did not pridefully attach degrees of importance to their tasks. They were not competing. They gratefully accepted their assignments as opportunities to glorify God—"Lord, you have assigned me my portion and my cup . . ." (Psalm 16:5). Years later, Elizabeth's son demonstrated humility when he said, "After me will come one who is more powerful than I, whose sandals I am not fit to carry" (Matthew 3:11).

Mary's Son was the Essence of humility: "Who, being in very nature God, did not consider equality with God something to be grasped, but made himself nothing, taking the very nature of a servant, being made in human likeness. And being found in appearance as a man, he humbled himself and became obedient to death—even death on a cross!" (Philippians 2:6–8).

Security Replaces Possessiveness

When a woman brings to a relationship the expectation that the other woman will provide her meaning and purpose, the stage is set for possessiveness. When a woman's ultimate identity is wrapped up in her abilities, circumstances, or relationships, she will derive her significance and security from these factors. She will fiercely cling to them in order to maintain her identity.

Generally, relationships are more important to women than things or circumstances. We are good at attaching. But this strength become a weakness if we become absorbed in the relationship. Once we cross that line, the relationship has to serve us, and we actually become a destructive force to that which is most precious to us. But that is just the point—it must never be the most precious thing to us because then it becomes our god.

Being someone else's god—her reason for being—is heavy stuff. Usually it seems that the only way out of a possessive relationship is to fight your way out. The possessive person clings with all her might to that which gives her significance or security. This is destructive to the one who is fighting to be released because she feels guilty. Unfortunately, it is this very characteristic that often prohibits biological mothers from being spiritual mothers. We are masters at masking our sin; our logic is that we cling because we care. The truth is that we cling because we are trying to get our security and significance from the wrong place.

When by grace we are freed from bondage to sin, we become free to enter into healthy relationships. When our security is in Jesus and our significance is in living for His glory, we are released from the need to possess.

Mary and Elizabeth enriched one another's life, but neither supplied the other's reason for being. They each defined themselves in terms of their relationship to God.

Appreciation Replaces Resentment

Resentment can take subtle forms in relationships between women, especially Christian women.

When older women are threatened by and resentful of younger women, they often cover it by trying to make themselves look better at the expense of the younger women. This happens when older women criticize the choices of younger women: "The younger women aren't concerned about helping with our projects or attending our meetings at church." Resentment also shows up in the form of comparisons: "The women today are too frivolous—we didn't have it as easy as they do, and we made it." Women who resent their own aging are often threatened by younger women. Rather than seeing the changes

---

The truth is that we cling [to our children] because we are trying to get our security and significance from the wrong place.

---

in themselves as signs to move into a different life-stage, they fight against those changes. This sets up conflicts within themselves as well as with others. This kind of attitude flies in the face of everything Paul told Titus to teach the older women to be. Although this is difficult today because the world puts such a premium on youth, God puts great value on the wisdom and discernment of the elderly:

> Rise in the presence of the aged, show respect for the elderly and revere your God. I am the LORD. (Leviticus 19:32)

> Gray hair is a crown of splendor; it is attained by a righteous life. (Proverbs 16:31)

Younger women often resent the "posture" of older women in the church. They think the older women have taken the position, "We did our time—now let the younger ones do the work." The younger women want an involvement with older women, but this translates into wanting the older women to "do" rather than appreciating what they are. The result is that older women feel the disapproval of the younger women and they back further away. Younger women also show immaturity when they resent the "pace" of older women. This manifests itself in remarks such as "They aren't interested in the same things we are—I have nothing in common with the older women."

Women in different seasons of life need to appreciate and value their own life-stage as well as the life-stage of other women. I believe when older women begin to retreat from activity, it is not a sign of unconcern about God's kingdom—it may simply be a sign that they do not have the energy to assume the same kind of responsibility and activity they once did. But another thing I have learned from observing these women is that they have more time and energy for prayer and meditating on God's Word. Many of these women are widows; many live alone. They have entered into a dimension of dependence on God that can only come when you are alone. What a waste if we miss the value of this life-stage by resenting them if they "do" fewer activities. When the life-stage of these women is appreciated they can become the prayer warriors and encouragers for younger women.

Resentment erects barriers that cause older and younger women to miss each other. Resentment is a product of a self-centered approach: Unless you are doing and being what I want you to do and be I am offended. Living for God's glory frees us to value and appreciate rather than resent one another. We can appreciate our diversity of temperaments, life-stages, life-situations, abilities, and callings from God. We don't have to be or do the same thing. In fact, there can be no real unity without diversity. Two of the same things don't need to blend to become one.

Mary and Elizabeth were two individual women at different life-stages and with different callings from God—with something essential in common, a desire to glorify God. They could appreciate and enjoy their diversity because of this life-purpose.

The sons of Mary and Elizabeth also had different callings. The followers of Elizabeth's son became concerned that Jesus was baptizing and that "everyone is going to him" (John 3:26). After all, John was the baptizer. John dispelled any resentment or jealously they were feeling with his classic statement: "He must become greater; I must become less" (John 3:30).

A Legacy of Trust

These radical differences in relating are only possible when women are living for God's glory. They may be at different levels of growth and development, but they are going in the same direction. In fact, the spiritual mother-daughter relationship implies that one is farther along in the application of this life-purpose. That is why she can encourage and equip the younger woman.

It is not enough for me to want to live for God's glory and for you to want to live for God's glory. I must want to help you live for God's glory. I must honestly want God's glory for your life. Now this is risky. It may well mean that the younger woman I dearly love will have to go through difficult times to be stripped of those things that hinder selfless living. I find that the more I love a younger woman, the more I want to protect and shield her. It is a constant discipline for me to stay out of the way. Encouraging and equipping is not the same as pampering and indulging. I am not to fix everything in the younger woman's life, nor am I to remove all of the tough times. This is easier said than done! It takes faith to tell a woman to lay aside self and become a servant. Does God's way really work?

Our daughter and her husband recently went through a period of unemployment. This was far more difficult for me than when my husband and I went through the same experience. It required enormous discipline for me to let her learn the precious lessons I had learned. It took God's wisdom to show me how to encourage and equip. We were continually faced with questions such as, "Do we pay this bill or let them pray it through?" I have to be honest and say that it took more discipline and wisdom than I had. My very wise husband helped me to trust God and risk putting our children into His loving care.

Even as I was writing this chapter, the telephone rang and I took a break to chat with Kathryn. During the conversation, I shared some of the thoughts the Lord had given me for this chapter. She said, "I'm glad I was forced out of my infant world view. Financial uncertainty pushed me into greater dependence on God. I had to put truths that I had heard all my life into practice. I learned firsthand about God's faithfulness." This mother's heart sang for joy! Seeing Kathryn realize God's grace

---

Encouraging and equipping is not the same as pampering and indulging.

---

experientially was far grander than any treasure this world could offer. And I could very easily have held her back from all God had for her.

Two women who are absorbed with God's glory are free from the self-saturation that characterizes our culture. These women can make a difference in one another's lives and in the lives of those they touch. Mary and Elizabeth were richer because of their relationship, and women through the ages have been encouraged and equipped to live for God's glory by their example. They left us a legacy. We can do for one another what they have done for us:

> They entered into a covenant to seek the LORD, the God of their fathers, with all their heart and soul. (2 Chronicles 15:12)

❧   ❧   ❧

A Spiritual Mothering Challenge

1. Begin with prayer.
   a. Evaluate your world view. How big is your circle? Pray that you will view the world and your life from God's perspective.
   b. What is your attitude toward older women and younger women? Confess any resentment. Accept and appreciate their life-stage.

2. Do you have a teachable spirit? Are you willing to learn from other women? Go to an older woman and ask her to help you live for God's glory.

3. Do you have relationships with women in different life-stages? If not, widen your circle. Invite a younger and an older woman to lunch or for dessert and talk about how you can enrich one another.

PART THREE

THE METHOD

*We have been made holy through the sacrifice of the
body of Jesus Christ once for all. Day after day every
priest stands and performs his religious duties; again
and again he offers the same sacrifices, which can
never take away sins. But when this priest had
offered for all time one sacrifice for sins, he sat down
at the right hand of God. . . . The Holy Spirit
also testifies to us about this. . . .
Therefore, . . . since we have confidence to enter the
Most Holy Place by the blood of Jesus, by a new and
living way opened for us through the curtain, that is,
his body, and since we have a great priest over the
house of God, let us draw near to God with a sincere
heart in full assurance of faith, having our hearts
sprinkled to cleanse us from a guilty conscience and
having our bodies washed with pure water. Let us
hold unswervingly to the hope we profess, for he who
promised is faithful. And let us consider how we may
spur one another on toward love and good deeds. Let
us not give up meeting together, as some are in the
habit of doing, but let us encourage one
another—and all the more as you
see the Day approaching.*

Hebrews 10:10–25

A Daughter's Story

Is there a need for spiritual mothering? There are not even words to express the depth of my affirmative answer to this question. You see, I am one of the walking wounded. And I suspect there are many, even within the church, who share my story and can identify with my pain. One of my earliest memories is coming home from school when I was six or seven and finding my mother in an unarousable state. She had attempted suicide. She had called a friend who arrived shortly after I did and called the ambulance.

My mother's parents are Christians. I think they sincerely tried to raise my mother, their only child, according to what they thought was right. But my mother rebelled against having "religion" forced on her. As far as I can tell, my mother's problems stem from her resentments toward her parents and the unacceptance and disapproval she felt from them. Some of these feelings are justified; some are not. Some may have been so magnified over time that it is difficult even for her to decipher what is real and what is imagined.

Whatever happened, my mother's unresolved conflicts with her own mother made her an emotional cripple. She has been a good mother in many ways, but she was never able to give me normal emotional support. There certainly was never any spiritual support. She taught me to be bitter and cynical. She told me never to trust anyone. She instilled a negative approach to life within me. I learned early not to tell her of my failures or problems because she sometimes took it personally and the rejection was too intense.

I became a Christian during my senior year in high school. That was sixteen years ago. Has it been that long? I think I should be more grown up. I know I am still trying to unlearn the lessons my mother taught me.

In the relearning process, I have found my identity in Jesus. I have experienced His forgiveness and, as far as I know my own heart, I have forgiven my mother. I have learned that God is sovereign and that He has a purpose in whom He gave me as parents. I believe there is a purpose for the hurt and the pain. I'm learning not to envy women who have loving, supportive Christian mothers. But in all honesty sometimes the envy is still there. The pain is always close to the surface. And I am terrified of passing on to my daughter the lessons my mother taught me.

Why is this relationship still painful even now that I am a Christian? I think it is because every girl wants her mother to be her protector. We need emotional nurturing just as desperately as we need physical nurturing. When we don't receive it, there are after-effects of malnutrition. There is a sense in which the pain became greater after I became a Christian. Before, I did not know that my experience had been abnormal. But after I tasted the pureness of Christian mothering, a desire was created that cannot be satisfied with anything less that what is true, lovely, pure, and holy.

The pain is ongoing because my mother and grand-mother use me as a pawn in their power struggle with each other. They each try to get me on "their side." Even if I insist on remaining neutral, they put me in the middle of their verbal brawls. I am torn between wanting to be a good daughter, yet returning from a visit emotionally spent. The pain is intensified because I know it could and should be different.

Anyone looking at me may assume that my life is wonderful. My husband is a successful professional; we have four beautiful children and a lovely home. Some may even consider me aloof. The truth is that it is sometimes very difficult for me to reach out to others. I plead with women not to make assumptions.

What do I need from other women? Most especially I crave the kind of relationship with an older woman who would be a "spiritual mother" to me. Someone who could teach me right from wrong, truth from lies; someone who could help me learn a Biblical perspective in all areas of life. That is asking a lot. That role usually is best filled by an older, more mature woman with greater experience in life and living. I wish it could be my own mother, but she is not able, and I will accept that.

I may be walking wounded, but by God's grace, I am more than a survivor. I am an overcomer. I will continue to move on in the warmth and light of my Heavenly Father's love and acceptance. Older women can, however, make the journey easier for women like me. And I hope to make it easier for other women.

Name withheld to protect my mother

8

THE MINISTRY
OF ENCOURAGEMENT

Encourage one another and build each other up.
1 Thessalonians 5:11

J ennifer was verbally and physically abused by her mother. Her parents divorced when Jennifer was ten because her father became involved with her mother's best friend. I could understand when she said, "I have always disliked and been afraid of women. What my mother did to me, and what her best friend did to her, made me fearful of friendships with women. When I became a Christian two years ago, I had absolutely no clue what it meant to be a Christian woman." Then Jennifer shared with me how she was invited to a women's Bible study. She told me of the love and acceptance she experienced there. She was so encouraged and strengthened by the women that her fears gradually dissolved. "The women created a safe place for me," she observed. "My relationship with my Heavenly Father soared. As I learned to trust Him, I learned to trust others. I am so grateful for those women and for the safety I feel with them."

Paul told Titus to teach the older women so that they could train the younger women. As we have already seen, one aspect of the Greek word *sophronizo*, translated "train," is to encourage. Encouragement is an important part of our spiritual mothering definition:

When a woman of faith and spiritual maturity enters into a nurturing relationship with a younger woman in order to encourage and equip her to live for God's glory.

Encouraging and equipping are necessary for effectual spiritual mothering. The two go together; to separate them diffuses both. Encouragement is the context in which equipping can take place. To equip apart from an atmosphere of encouragement is rigid and formal, impersonal and cold.

Entering into the ministry of encouragement is not just an exercise in fluff. The ministry of encouragement is hard work and can only be carried out properly if it is based upon sound doctrine. We must understand what Scripture says about encouragement in order to be encouragers.

The Foundation of Our Ministry

The foundation of the ministry of encouragement is the finished work of Jesus Christ.

> We have been made holy through the sacrifice of the body of Jesus Christ once for all. Day after day every priest stands and performs his religious duties; again and again he offers the same sacrifices, which can never take away sins. But when this priest had offered for all time one sacrifice for sins, he sat down at the right hand of God. . . . The Holy Spirit also testifies to us about this. (Hebrews 10:10–15)

The author states his case that the once-for-all sacrifice of Jesus completed His work on our behalf. Then he gives a powerful therefore:

> Therefore, . . . since we have confidence to enter the Most Holy Place by the blood of Jesus . . . and since we have a great priest over the house of God, . . . (Hebrews 10:19–21)

Because of the completed work of Christ, we have access to the very presence of God—and we can actually enter that Holy Place with confidence. Confidence in His finished work takes us into the Holy Place of prayer and fellowship with Him where we receive confidence to go out and serve Him. So the writer continues the *therefore* as he lists several things we are to do.

Encouragement is the context in which equipping can take place.

But remember, it is the vertical relationship that originates with God that frees and enables us to do the things required in the following list:

- let us draw near to God . . .
- let us hold unswervingly to the hope we profess . . .

- let us consider how we may spur one another on toward love and good deeds . . .
- let us not give up meeting together . . .
- let us encourage one another and all the more as you see the Day approaching. (Hebrews 10:23–25)

The first grouping "let us" imperatives refers to our relationship with God and encourages us to continue moving towards Him. The second grouping refers to our association with other believers and tells us to give careful thought as to how we can urge one another on in the same direction that we are moving. The implication is that if we are not moving in that direction, we cannot encourage others. The closer we get to God and the tighter we hold to the hope we have in Him, the more we are able to encourage and equip others to a life of love and good deeds.

The second "let us" grouping contains three elements: spurring one another on (equipping), meeting together (relationships), and encouragement. When Christ-followers meet together, encouragement and equipping in obedient living should be an outgrowth of that assembly. And we are not to expect it to just happen—we are to think about and plan for it. When the encourager/equipper (the spiritual mother) is following the example of the Master Teacher, the learner (spiritual daughter) will have increasing confidence to move on toward love and good deeds.

In *The Big Umbrella*, Dr. Jay E. Adams begins a description of the teaching ministry of Jesus with Mark 3:14:

> He appointed twelve—designating them apostles—that they might be with him and that he might send them out to preach.

Dr. Adams then explains that the key words are "with him." Jesus did not view teaching in the narrow sense of only imparting factual information. "There is also much more to teaching than the teaching of content. That is why the Bible does not say that Jesus appointed twelve that He might INSTRUCT them. He does not say that He appointed twelve that He might send them to class . . . That was all part of it, but, note, only a part."[1]

Dr. Adams then moves to Luke 6:40 where Jesus Himself defines the pupil-teacher relationship: "A student is not above his teacher, but everyone who is fully trained will be like his teacher."

He observes,

> Jesus did not say, "will THINK like his teacher." That is part of it, but, again, it is only part of it. Jesus said that a pupil who has been properly (fully) taught "will BE like his teacher." He will BE like him, not just THINK like him.[2]

Did Jesus' methodology work?

> After Jesus had risen from the dead and ascended into heaven, He sent His Spirit back to continue His work through the Church. In Acts 4:13, Luke gives us a view of how the enemies of the Church looked upon the disciples . . . When they saw the courage of Peter and John and realized that they were unschooled, ordinary men, they were astonished and they took note that these men had been with Jesus.[3]

The thing that astonished this religious body was the courage and confidence of these ordinary men. And they could not escape the fact that they had been with Jesus. Being *with* a spiritual mother who reflects Christ will encourage and equip a

---

Being with a spiritual mother who reflects Christ will encourage and equip a young woman to be like Him.

---

young woman to be *like* Him. This in turn will inspire courage and confidence in the younger woman that will astonish those who see the results in her life. But what is encouragement? What does it look like? How do we do it?

A Definition of Encouragement

The Greek word translated "encouragement" is *parakaleo*. This is from the same root word as *parakletos*, which means "called to one's aid" and is translated "Helper" in John 14:26:

> But the Helper, the Holy Spirit, whom the Father will send in My name, He will teach you all things, and bring to your remembrance all that I said to you. (NASB)

The exciting thing for our discussion is that when God created woman, He designed her to be a helper:

> The Lord God said, "It is not good for the man to be alone. I will make a helper [ezer] suitable for him." (Genesis 2:18)

I certainly do not want to imply that men are not to be helpers/encouragers. The many Scriptural exhortations about encouragment apply to all believers. However, it does seem that women have been uniquely designed and equipped for the ministry of helper/encourager. Women's nurturing instincts and helper-design do give an edge that perhaps make it easier and more natural.

Being a helper/encourager is not a secondary role. Throughout the Old Testament, God is referred to as our *ezer* (Exodus 18:4, Deuteronomy 33:29, Psalm 20:2, Psalm 70:5, and others). Two of the references are especially compelling:

> The victim commits himself to you; you are the helper of the fatherless. (Psalm 10:14)

> For He will deliver the needy who cry out, the afflicted who have no one to help. (Psalm 72:12)

The victims, the fatherless, the needy, and the afflicted of our day are crying out for help and encouragement. Many of these are young women who desperately need spiritual mothers to encourage and equip them to live for God's glory. Words of encouragement can pump spiritual adrenalin into their souls.

The *American Heritage Dictionary* gives a good definition of encouragement that is consistent with what the Bible teaches us about this ministry: "To inspire to continue on a chosen course; impart courage or confidence to; embolden; hearten. To give support to."

Encouragement in Action

When God's people assemble, whether it is for Sabbath worship, a women's Bible study, or two women having lunch together, there should be an atmosphere of encouragement. Women are skilled at creating ambiance. It is no secret that women set the tone and mood of a home—both by their attitudes and their actions. Perhaps this is why the writer of Proverbs said: "The wise woman builds her house, but with her own hands the foolish one tears hers down" (Proverbs 14:1).

The wise woman will have a building influence in her relationships; a foolish woman will have a destructive influence in her relationships. And this influence extends beyond the home to every part of her life where she has the opportunity to affect the atmosphere. A church that has the combination of sound preaching from the pulpit and a unified effort of encouragement from the pews will be dynamite! And I personally believe that it is primarily women who bring the energy of encouragement into a church.

The encouragement imperative tells us to ". . . consider how we may spur one another on toward love and good deeds." To understand how to put this into practice, visualize a cave with people hiding inside. This represents people hiding their spiritual gifts. It is impossible to "spur them on to love and good deeds" when they are hiding.

But why are they hiding? Usually the assumption is made that these people are not committed to the Lord or to the ministry of the church. Their non-involvement is interpreted as lack of commitment. Of course the commitment level is sometimes a problem. But more often, the problem is not lack of commitment but lack of confidence.

Generally, people are in the cave because that is the safest place to be, or at least, they perceive it to be the safest place. Involvement necessitates vulnerability that is risky. What if I fail? What if I don't meet the expectations of others? What if I'm criticized or rejected? Most of us simply are not willing to take that kind of risk unless we are operating in a safe environment.

God provides safety for His people. We should seek to do the same.

> For in the day of trouble he will keep me safe in his dwelling; he will hide me in the shelter of his tabernacle and set me high upon a rock. (Psalm 27:5)
>
> Serve one another in love. (Galatians 5:13)

We must make it safer for people to be *outside* of the cave than it is to be *inside* the cave. And God tells us how to do this: "let us not give up meeting together . . . let us encourage one another." Encouraging relationships can make it safe for people to come out of the cave and to use their spiritual gifts "for the common good" (1 Corinthians 12:7).

The process of creating a safe environment begins with serving in love, and we are commanded to do this: "Serve one another in love" (Galations 5:13). Remember the example of Jesus doing the task of a servant when He washed the disciples' feet? Serving in love demands being stripped of self. It is not just serving—that would be difficult enough—it is serving in love.

Serving in love may simply take the form of giving a hug and a word of encouragement to young mothers who make the effort to get themselves and their children to church on Sunday. It may mean reaching out to a young women who has become withdrawn and inviting her to lunch. It may mean taking a meal to a young woman because you detect unusual fatigue. It may mean laying aside your own plans to enjoy an afternoon alone when a young woman calls and asks for your help in working through struggles she is experiencing in her marriage. It may mean expressing admiration to a young woman who desires to be married but who is determined to only date Christians—and there seem to be no prospects.

"Miss" Forrestine is in her seventies. She has never been married. She is a sprightly little woman, less than five feet tall, but she is a spiritual giant to the young women in our church. She nurtures them by her love and her example.

Immediately after the worship service on Sunday mornings, Forrestine hurries out. She stands just outside the door with a bag of candy for the children. When I asked her why she does this, she said, "When I first started, there were only a few children in the church. I wanted to encourage them. Even though now there are lots of children, I just keep doing it. I guess I do it because I love them."

The mothers of these children know that Forrestine loves them. They know they can look to her for wise advice; they can depend on her to pray for them, and they can count on her to babysit. Recently, I heard one of the young women tell her, "Miss Forrestine, it meant so much to me for you to be beside me at the pro-life rally last week. This is an issue that is so important to those of us who are in the mothering stage of life, and it was such an encouragement for you to be there."

Forrestine is an activist. She writes letters to companies and congressmen about issues affecting the family. She uses neither her age nor her singleness as an excuse for inactivity. She sees her retirement and no family responsibilities as opportunities for service.

We serve in love as we pray for sensitivity to the needs of others and reach out to meet those needs in positive and practical ways. As this happens, we move to the second stage in the

---

Most women are able to move quickly and easily beyond the superficial and on to a personal level in their relationships. We are comfortable with attachments.

---

process which Paul describes as being "knit together in love" (Colossians 2:2, NASB). According to the dictionary, to knit means "to join closely; unite securely."

The connecting of lives through serving in love is one of the most powerful aspects of the Christian community. This "close joining" characterizes women's friendships. We are not satisfied with surface friendships. Most women are able to move quickly and easily beyond the superficial and on to a personal level in their relationships. We are comfortable with attachments. Emotional intimacy is important to us and "unites securely" our friendships.

As the threads of lives are knit together, they become so interwoven that an environment of security is created. When fear is removed, there is freedom to serve. The security of the relationship becomes a safer place than the aloneness of the cave. The light of encouragement instills the courage and confidence a woman needs to come out of the cave. Then she can be equipped to use her spiritual gifts "for the common good," and the church is enriched.

If we reverse the process—if we insist on equipping before we have encouraged—we drive women deeper into the cave. Love motivates. Guilt devastates.

Again, this is hard work. It is not shallow sentimentality. The ministry of encouragement is grounded on what God has done for us in Christ. He has clearly communicated to us that the Holy Place—His presence—is now a safe place for us because Jesus opened the way. The encouragment we receive in this safe place produces the confidence and the ability to be encouragers. This is not confidence in our own ability. This is confidence in God and ability that grows out of being in that Holy Place. Our relationships with younger women cannot and should not duplicate completely the safety and security that we have in our relationship with our Father. However, we must give careful thought to how our relationships with them can encourage them to find their safety and security in Him.

> Strengthen the feeble hands, steady the knees that give way;
> say to those with fearful hearts, "Be strong, do not fear; your
> God will come . . . he will come to save you." (Isaiah 35:3–4)

When we invest in encouraging other women, we will have the glorious experience of seeing them come out of the cave and use their spiritual gifts for God's glory. They will have confidence to reach out to others. The result: creative, nurturing ministries of love and good deeds. Encouragement by other women is probably the most effective and efficient way to tap the rich resource of the female population of a local church.

Each week in our women's Bible study, older and younger women are paired as prayer partners. They are encouraged to minister to each other during the week. One week, during sharing time, three of the young women told about being invited, along with their pre-school children, to Margaret's home for lunch. During the previous weeks, Margaret had been paired with each of these women. The young women were joyously animated as they told about the delightful time they had getting to know Margaret and one another.

If we reverse the process—if we insist on equipping before we have encouraged—we drive women deeper into the cave. Love motivates. Guilt devastates.

After listening to their glowing account of the day, I looked at Margaret and said, "And how did you feel about this event?" This seventy-ish widow's eyes twinkled as she said, "I had so much fun, and that night I slept like a baby!" Since that time, there has been a steady stream of young women to Margaret's home. Margaret has discovered a ministry. And are the young women encouraged? For sure!

 za   za   za

1. Begin with prayer.

   a. Meditate on Hebrews 10:10–25. Spend time praising God for the confidence you have in approaching Him because of what Jesus has done for you.

   b. Are you an encourager? Do you encourage your husband, children, co-workers, friends? Which is safer, being in the cave or being with you?

   c. Are you discouraged? Do you need encouragement? Reflect on Psalm 10:16–18.

2. Ask God to give you a sensitivity toward one younger woman that you can begin serving in love. Does she need a babysitter, a note of encouragement, or an invitation to lunch? Be careful not to "urge" her toward love and good deeds until you have cultivated the relationship by serving her in love.

3. If you are a younger woman wanting encouragement from an older woman, commit this desire to your Father. Then go to an older woman who reflects Christ, and tell her that you see Him in her. She will be encouraged, and you will have the beginning of an encouraging relationship.

4. Call an older woman and ask for her advice about something. It can be anything from asking how to cook a pot-roast to how to be an encourager to your husband. She will feel valued, and you will get some wise advice.

Georgia's Story

I took my place beside my husband to greet people as they left the sanctuary on Sunday morning. I always looked forward to this time of exchanging hugs, handshakes, and news of prayers answered and prayers needed. One of the first to come by was usually a special friend named Gracie. She would shake our hands and then linger near by to lovingly greet everyone.

Gracie was elderly, short and plump, not an attractive person as the world judges. But Gracie drew people to her and to the church by her love. Gracie "grandmothered" the whole church. She gave unconditional love to each one and always expected the best of us and for us.

On Sunday morning at the door, she might whisper in my ear, "Stand up straight." With a twinkle at my husband, she would say, "I didn't go to sleep this morning." Every child that came by would give Gracie a hug, and Gracie would call them by name. She was in her eighties, but the year before she died, there were twenty some babies born to the church family, and she knew their names. Each one was someone new for Gracie to love.

A number of young bachelors in the church counted Gracie among their special friends and prayer partners. It was not unusual to see her leaving the church on Sunday morning on the arm of a young man who was taking her to lunch. If Gracie was absent from any church service, we knew that she was either ill or did not have a ride. And several were sure to call her that day.

All of us relied on Gracie's prayers. We could count on her to talk to the Lord and not to other people about our problems. Her death left a hole in that congregation that was much larger than Gracie. By her life, she showed me the power of unconditional love and convinced me that every church needs a woman who will be a "spiritual grandmother" to the congregation. One like that cannot be hired; she is a special gift of God to His people.

Georgia Settle
Rosman, North Carolina

9

THE POWER
OF ACCEPTANCE

*May the God who gives endurance and encouragement give
you a spirit of unity among yourselves as you follow Christ
Jesus, so that with one heart and mouth you may glorify the
God and Father of our Lord Jesus Christ. Accept one
another, then, just as Christ accepted you,
in order to bring praise to God.*

Romans 15:5–7

I t was one of those "divine connections." I could not have
planned or orchestrated it. So many women attended the
meeting where I was speaking, but suddenly I was standing
alone with one woman. Lori seemed surprised not only at the
unusual circumstance but also at her openness as she began to
tell me her story. "It was hard for me to come to this meeting. I
have been a member of this church for several years, but I am
not involved in the women's ministry. The women in this
church are so godly, if they knew about my past they could
never accept me." Then Lori told me about having an abortion
when she was in college. We arranged a time to get together
later.

As I talked with her, I agreed that the women in her
church were indeed women of beautiful spiritual depth; however, I explained that because of that spirituality I was confident they would not reject her. Seeing that I did not reject her
gave her confidence to share with one of the women in her

church. This woman accepted and loved Lori. Lori became involved in the women's ministry and eventually "went public" and shared her testimony at their Bible study. Acceptance by other women freed Lori to establish meaningful relationships with these women. But that's not the end of the story. Their acceptance also pumped confidence in her to use her experience to minister to other postabortal women. That's the power of acceptance.

How do we do it? How do we show acceptance of women in such a way as to encourage them? What qualities should a spiritual mother embody and teach to a younger woman?

Scripture tells us of a woman who had a dramatic impact on her local church. How she did this is an intriguing illustration of encouraging others by accepting them.

> In Joppa there was a disciple named Tabitha (which, when translated, is Dorcas), who was always doing good and helping the poor. . . . she became sick and died. . . . when the disciples heard that Peter was in Lydda, they sent two men to him and urged him, "Please come at once!"
>
> Peter went with them, and when he arrived, he was taken upstairs to the room. All the widows stood around him, crying and showing him the robes and other clothing that Dorcas had made while she was still with them.
>
> Peter sent them all out of the room; then he got down on his knees and prayed. Turning toward the dead woman, he said, "Tabitha, get up." She opened her eyes and seeing Peter she sat up. He took her by the hand and helped her to her feet. Then he called the believers and the widows and presented her to them alive. This became known all over Joppa, and many people believed in the Lord. (Acts 9:36–42)

Dorcas is one of my all-time favorite women in the church. Her contemporary counterparts are also women that I admire greatly. What is it about Dorcas, and women like her, that arouse such admiration? A close look at the episode in Joppa provides an example of a powerful relational skill: encouragement through acceptance.

Meeting Real Needs of Real People

In the Scripture passage above, we learn that when Dorcas died there was such a crisis in the Joppa congregation that two men were sent to Lydda to urge Peter to "come at once!" Now this is interesting in light of the kind of ministry that Dorcas had. You will notice that there is no mention that she was a dynamic teacher or that she was a large contributor of funds or that she led a growing discipleship group. Doing good and helping the poor are admirable, but this hardly seems to be the type minis-

> ***Dorcas must have been highly organized and structured to have been able to "do good and help the poor" all year long, not just at Christmas.***

try that would be highlighted in the church's yearly report. Dorcas was not involved in a highly visible ministry, and yet her death created a major crisis. Surely other people in the congregation had died. Why did this death necessitate an immediate dispatch to Peter?

There is an element of speculation here, but it seems that Dorcas carried out a ministry of caring that met real needs of real people. Apparently, she did it in such a way that others were built up and encouraged, not pressured or discouraged. "Always doing good and helping the poor" is quite an inclusive statement. If I am really honest, I have to admit that the word "always" causes some discomfort to bubble up in me. This woman must have been highly organized and structured to have been able to "do good and help the poor" all year long, not just at Christmas.

The reason I feel some discomfort is that, like many women, I have to battle the super-woman syndrome. Many of the messages women hear today tell us that we must have it all and do it all—and be good at it. What's more, we must look good while we're doing it! Something about our femaleness makes us feel that we must measure up to our often inflated perception of what we think our families, our churches, and society expect from us. We inflict enormous pressure on ourselves. So when a woman comes along who appears to be a superwoman, the pressure is intensified. In the Christian community, a woman who is "always" doing good can definitely create a problem if she gives the impression that she is disappointed or discouraged with our level of ministry-performance. The person who projects this attitude is described by Marshall Shelley as a well-intentioned dragon:

> Within the church, they are often sincere, well-meaning saints, but they leave ulcers, strained relationships, and hard feelings in their wake. They don't consider themselves difficult people. They don't sit up nights thinking of ways to be nasty. Often they are pillars of the community—talented, strong personalities, deservingly respected—but for some reason, they undermine the ministry of the church. They are not naturally rebellious or pathological; they are loyal church members, convinced they're serving God, but they wind up doing more harm than good.[1]

A dragon is characterized by the fire that comes from its mouth; dragons in the church are known by the burning words they utter. Their words and attitudes wound and destroy and cause considerable anxiety for those around them because they set a "spiritual" standard for themselves and then impose it on everyone else. And no one measures up. Dragons do not accept the limitations or preferences of anyone who is not in full agreement with them.

What do these dragons do? They write critical letters to the pastor or elders of the church. A female dragon can be heard insinuating that if the other women in the church would just help with the clothes closet ministry, she would not be so overworked. She also complains that the deacons are not really concerned about the poor, or they would budget more money for the project. Female dragons criticize the younger women in the church for attending pro-life rallies rather than learning to sew.

It is sad but true that when a dragon is removed from a congregation, even though he/she had been a hard worker who zealously served the Lord, there is often a sigh of relief rather than a crisis!

But Dorcas was not a dragon. She shows us that it is possible to be an intelligent, organized woman who is deeply involved in ministry without making others feel guilty or pressured.

Charity Enveloped in Love

What was it about Dorcas that made her such a beloved elect lady? As I have reflected on the character and ministry of this woman, I have come to believe that her power was in her person. First and foremost, Dorcas was a disciple of Jesus. This is the first thing we learn about her from the Scripture passage. In fact, she must have been a very disciplined disciple to have had such a far-reaching ministry. But her ministry was not one of duty; it was a ministry of love. Because her deeds of charity were an expression of God's grace in her life, they were enveloped with love. An attitude of love for Jesus and acceptance of others must have so permeated her actions that she posed no threat to other women or to men.

As I observe modern-day daughters of Dorcas, I see in their actions what I imagine was true of Joppa's Dorcas:

I can imagine Dorcas enthusiastically welcoming a newcomer in the congregation and inviting her for tea. I can imagine her listening to the woman and learning about her loneliness and insecurity, and then assessing her gifts and circumstances and gently asking if perhaps she would have time to help hem some garments. I can imagine Dorcas being very careful not to place demands on the woman but to communicate a belief in the woman's potential. I can imagine Dorcas convincing the woman that she had never seen robes hemmed so beautifully and then inviting the woman to go along as she delivered the gift. I can imagine Dorcas cautiously stretching the woman so that confidence was built, but guilt was never imposed. And I can imagine this woman soon venturing out on her own ministry. I can imagine a delighted Dorcas approaching another woman whom she had observed to have organizational gifts and asking if she would be interested in mobilizing some of the young mothers and their children to deliver meals to the poor.

I can imagine women of all ages in the congregation receiving notes of appreciation and encouragement from Dorcas.

I can imagine Dorcas asking the newly widowed or recently divorced woman to sit with her in church and then inviting her for lunch.

I can imagine Dorcas greeting a first-time visitor to the church, learning something about them, and jotting down their name. Then the following week, she would greet them by name and introduce them to someone else so that they would begin to feel "at home." A Dorcas works hard to create a "family atmosphere" in her church.

I can imagine Dorcas taking a special interest in the pastor's wife and children as she frequently expressed appreciation for their willingness to share their husband/daddy with the congregation. Dorcas also writes notes to the pastor and elders of the church, but they are notes of appreciation and encouragement.

I can imagine Dorcas talking with a young woman who is disappointed in her marriage. Perhaps the young woman feels lonely because her husband is not as attentive as she would like for him to be—or she feels frustrated because he does not have the same approach to finances she has—or she doubts his spiritual depth. Dorcas would gently guide the young women to see that her lack of acceptance of her husband is creating a barrier to his growth and development. Perhaps Dorcas would say, "A wife's responsibility is to make her husband happy. It is God's responsibility to make him holy. And a happy husband is more open to becoming a holy husband." Dorcas, as I perceive her, is very practical. She would explain to young women that meeting the sexual need of a man communicates acceptance more powerfully than anything else. And a man needs to feel accepted by his wife.

I can imagine Dorcas lovingly but firmly challenging the empty-nester woman, who complains about boredom, that there is kingdom work to be done and offering to help her get involved in ministry. Dorcas would lovingly share some of her thoughts about making lists every night so that you have goals for the next day rather than living purposeless, soap-opera filled days. But when a young mother expressed frustration that she

> **I can imagine Dorcas lovingly but firmly challenging the empty-nester woman, who complains about boredom, that there is kingdom work to be done and offering to help her get involved in ministry.**

could not be involved in ministry, I can imagine Dorcas reminding her that there are different seasons of life and that her mission field is her home at this stage of life.

I can imagine women often hearing the words "I'll pray about that" from Dorcas. And somehow they knew that she really would—perhaps they believed it because of the little notebook that she immediately opened and scribbled a reminder, or perhaps they knew because she periodically asked about the situation.

I can imagine everyone feeling loved when they were with Dorcas.

I can imagine everyone feeling accepted, even the teenagers with their crazy hairstyles and outlandish clothes. Somehow, they didn't feel it made any difference to Dorcas. Mothers of those teenagers were also comfortable around Dorcas because she talked about how wonderful it was that the church had so many young people rather than wondering where their parents had gone wrong.

All of these "imaginings" are not the result of a vivid imagination. They are what I have seen in modern-day daughters of Dorcas in local churches throughout the country. I can spot a contemporary Dorcas even when I visit in a church I have never attended. There are always people around her. Sometimes they are laughing—sometimes you see tears. She has a smile, a hug, and a kind word for everybody. Is it any wonder that the death of a Dorcas creates a vacuum in a church?

People aren't afraid of a Dorcas. They are not intimidated by her. It's safe to be with a Dorcas.

Unity Through Acceptance

But now for the exciting conclusion to the Dorcas drama. Peter went to Joppa. God raised Dorcas from the dead, and Peter "presented her to them alive"—God's gift to the Joppa congregation. As a result, many people believed in the Lord. Now what was this all about? Did God change His mind about the timing of Dorcas' death? Of course not!

The death of Dorcas was designed by a sovereign God to demonstrate His love and His power to the church in Joppa. This demonstration required the removal of a person who was greatly loved and whose ministry touched the lives of the people in that church. And God chose a woman. Not just any woman but a disciple who patterned her life after the One she followed. Dorcas had experienced the encouragement that comes in knowing she had been accepted by Christ; this motivated her to accept others. Dorcas had a unifying effect in her church; God is glorified when believers are unified. And unity is impossible apart from acceptance:

> May the God who gives endurance and encouragement give you a spirit of unity among yourselves as you follow Christ Jesus, so that with one heart and mouth you may glorify the God and Father of our Lord Jesus Christ. Accept one an-

other, then, just as Christ accepted you, in order to bring praise to God. (Romans 15:5–7)

Believers can have confidence to approach God because we have been accepted by Him. We have been accepted because of the work of Christ on our behalf. We in turn must extend ac-

---

Dorcas exemplifies spiritual mothering. But can such a low-profile woman really make a difference today as we confront the problems of our modern culture?

---

ceptance to one another. We must be approachable. But people can only approach us with confidence if we have communicated acceptance. It is impossible to encourage one you have not accepted. An attitude of acceptance must be communicated by our words and deeds.

Failure to accept another reveals pride in my own heart: "I know what you should be, what you should do, and how you should do it—my way is right and best." It also reveals lack of trust: "God is not changing you fast enough, so I must help Him."

Dorcas is a commentary on serving in love—becoming knit together in love—and creating an environment where others are stimulated to love and good deeds. Dorcas made a difference in the lives of those around her. Dorcas exemplifies spiritual mothering.

But can such a low-profile woman really make a difference today as we confront the problems of our modern culture? Consider the following report:

Fewer than 10 percent of Americans are deeply committed Christians, but they're particularly influential and happy, according to pollster George Gallup. He gave an urban ministries conference some preliminary highlights from the report, "The Saints Among Us," indicating only about 6 to 10 percent have what he termed a "high spiritual faith." "These people are a breed apart," he said. "They are more tolerant of people of diverse backgrounds. They are more involved in charitable activities. They are more involved in practical Christianity. They are absolutely committed to prayer." Additionally, he said, they are "far, far happier than the rest of the population." These are the quiet saints in our society who have a disproportionate, powerful impact on our communities.[2]

A Dorcas can make a difference. But is there a need for a Dorcas in today's church? Dr. James Dobson addressed this in his book *Straight Talk to Men and Their Wives*. In commenting on the increase in depression and loneliness among women, he contends that the breakdown today is not between men and women, but between women and women.

A century ago, women cooked together, canned together, washed at the creek together, prayed together, went through menopause together, and grew old together. And when a baby was born, aunts and grandmothers and neighbors were there to show the new mother how to diaper and feed and discipline. Great emotional support was provided in this feminine contact. A woman was never really alone.

Alas, the situation is very different today. The extended family has disappeared, depriving the wife of that source of security and fellowship. Her mother lives in New Jersey and her sister is in Texas. Furthermore, American families move every three or four years, preventing any long-term friendships from developing among neighbors.[3]

The mobility of our society and the pluralism of our culture increase the need for supportive networks for women. The church is the logical place for Christian women to connect with other women of faith. Relevant women's ministries can put these networks in place that will help construct a female-friendly church.

Daughters of Dorcas, stand up and be counted. By encouraging and equipping younger women to live for God's glory, we can have a disproportionate, powerful impact upon them. But to do this, we must encourage them by accepting them—and we must teach them to do the same.

❧   ❧   ❧

A Spiritual Mothering Challenge

1. Begin with prayer.
   a. Meditate on Romans 15:5–7 and praise God for the encouragement you receive from Him. Thank Him that Christ has accepted you.
   b. Examine your "acceptance attitude." Do you communicate loving acceptance to other women? Are you approachable? Do the people in your church know that you love them?

2. Read again the list of things I "imagine" Dorcas doing and then be a contemporary Dorcas by putting one of my "imaginings" into action.

3. Invite a single woman to have dinner with your family. Most single women long for opportunities to be with a family.

A Daughter's Story

My mother is loyal, strong, affectionate, and ever ready to defend one who she feels is treated unjustly. She is also bitter, angry, manipulative, and sometimes, dare I say it, just plain mean. Mother has many other characteristics to go along with these, but the ones named are the ones that come immediately to mind when I try to describe her. They also come to mind when I try to describe me. Remember—I am my mother's child.

When I listen to my friends who grew up in Christian homes talk about their childhood, I'm amazed. They sometimes sound as if they were reared by June and Ward Cleaver. While I know that their lives were not perfect, I also know that the mind's eye of my childhood looks a little more like "Roseanne" than "Leave It To Beaver." Get the picture?

One thing that I notice when I look back at childhood is that I didn't understand how bad it all was at the time. I accepted my lot in life as one who had never known anything different. I thought that all mommies loved their children when they were good and hated them when they had not lived up to expectations. I thought that all daughters were afraid of their mothers and worked very hard so that mother would have no cause for angry words. I thought that all mothers occasionally yelled, cursed, and slapped you in the face. Now, when I read the things I've written here, I'm shocked. Then, it was normal.

Now that you have read these things, I'm sure that you don't like my mother very much. She is not easy to like. Can we really blame her, though? She has only acted out what she was taught. Remember—she is her mother's child.

Maybe if someone, just one person, had loved Mother, unconditionally. Maybe if someone had taken the time to explain to Mother that God's acceptance and love are not based on performance. Could one person, making the sacrifice to get involved in the life of that young girl who was my mother, have made a difference? I think so.

One woman made a difference for me. She is not someone I would want to pattern my entire life after. We are now at very different places theologically. But, she was willing to give of herself, to get involved, to show me that the way of life that I accepted as normal was not all there was. My gracious God used that woman to show me Himself and to change the course of my life for eternity.

Since that time God has used many godly women (and a couple of men) to teach me more of His ways. Each one has had different things to offer—one gentleness, one sweet mothering, another generosity—all have offered that rare jewel: unconditional love.

I am reminded to be thankful—to be thankful that the chain is broken. The chain of bondage that ties my mother to bitterness and rage and fear is broken in me. My children, because of my past, will see glimpses of the chain, but they will not have to bear its weight. Because of the willingness of one woman to give of herself, my grandchildren will not have the sins of some long past ancestor to shed. Instead, God willing, they will have two generations of prayers to guide them.

The effects of spiritual mothering are not for one person alone, or even one generation. They are for eternity.

Soli Deo Gloria!

10

THE CORNERSTONE
OF FORGIVENESS

*Be kind and compassionate to one another,
forgiving each other, just as in Christ God forgave you.*
Ephesians 4:32

F orgiveness is the cornerstone of the ministry of encouragement, yet many believers are blocked from experiencing
the joy of their salvation and from being encouragers to others
because of an unforgiving spirit. We must examine this fundamental and indispensable part of the Christian life with great
care and gentleness. For the person who has been deeply
wounded, it is difficult to cut through the pain and to consider
whether or not she has forgiven the one who inflicted the
wounds.

Dear reader, please know that I approach this topic with
much prayer. I am not going to glibly say, "If you really forgive
you will forget." I will say that I am grateful for every opportunity I have had to forgive. I am not saying I am grateful for the
pain—that would be sadistic. I am grateful for opportunities to
forgive because extending forgiveness necessitated drinking
deeper of God's grace than any other act of obedience.

I have seen what forgiveness and unforgiveness look like.
Forgiveness is beautiful. Unforgiveness is ugly. Julia and Sarah
are sisters. They are both in their sixties. I met Julia first. I was
immediately attracted to this lively woman. My first impression
was of her quickness to detect and respond to hesitant, with-

drawn women. She seemed to instinctively know they were hurting. The more I observed her, the more curious I was. I knew there had to be a "story" that had shaped this woman's radiance.

When I questioned her, she told me that she had been physically abused by her father. She remembered standing between her daddy and her younger sister as he pointed a pistol and threatened to kill them. "My healing came when I finally understood the price, extent, and power of God's forgiveness. No matter what my daddy did to me, it was not as offensive nor did it cost as much as my sin offended and cost my Heavenly Father." She told me that when her father was dying, she visited him, held his hand, and told him she loved him. He never asked for her forgiveness and never said he was sorry. But because of her Heavenly Father's forgiveness to her, she was able to forgive her earthly Father.

"What about your sister?" I asked. Her face saddened. "She would never forgive. She would not even go in the room to see him when he was dying. But what is even more tragic is that every relationship in her life is poisoned with her bitterness. Her anger spills over to her husband and to her children. She is a prisoner to her past."

When I met Sarah I was startled by the contrast. She looks much older than her older sister. There is a hardness about her that repels rather than the softness that draws people to Julia. Julia's life is beautiful. Sarah's life is ugly. The price of unforgiveness is high.

I have also seen what forgiveness looks like on the pages of Scripture. An intriguing Old Testament story has taught me much about forgiveness. Forgiveness is perhaps not the obvious lesson in this story, but I think it is the undercurrent that moves the story to its outcome. It is interesting that the woman in this story is described as beautiful.

In 1 Samuel 24 and 26 we read two extraordinary accounts of David extending kindness, compassion, and forgiveness to King Saul. But tucked between these two chapters is the fascinating story of David's near slip into revenge. It is against the darkness of this failure that the character of a godly woman brilliantly sparkles. David almost "lost it," but God graciously sent Abigail to intervene.

Breaking the Barrier of Unforgiveness

Let's recap the situation. David had fallen from the favored position of living in the palace and playing his harp to soothe King Saul's spirit, to being relentlessly pursued by the King and his army. David and his followers seldom had a moment's peace. Then there was the rather embarrassing experience when Saul

---

I am grateful for opportunities to forgive because extending forgiveness necessitated drinking deeper of God's grace than any other act of obedience.

---

went into a cave to "relieve himself." Saul was totally unaware that David and some of his men were "far back in the cave." David's men were ecstatic: "This is the day the LORD spoke of when he said to you, 'I will give your enemy into your hands for you to deal with as you wish'" (1 Samuel 24:3–4). David crept up and cut off a corner of Saul's robe but refused to touch the Lord's anointed. He even felt remorseful that he had cut Saul's robe. What restraint!

In the very next chapter, however, David sent ten young men to request food from a local farmer. When Nabal refused his request, David was furious. "Instead of overcoming evil with good, he was in imminent danger of being overcome with evil."[1] This glaring inconsistency is the backdrop of Abigail's story.

It should be noted that David's request to Nabal for food was legitimate. It was not unusual to ask for provisions from a fellow countryman. The request was made with respect, and it was reasonable for David to expect it to be honored. But Nabal was "surly and mean in his dealings." Notice the contrast with the description of his wife Abigail: "She was an intelligent and beautiful woman" (1 Samuel 25:3).

David was infuriated with Nabal's rude refusal and showed absolutely no restraint. He instructed his men to prepare their swords. David was so filled with spite that he intended to kill Nabal and all of his men.

Abigail was unaware of her husband's foolish actions, but Nabal's servants knew what he had done and they realized the potential danger. Significantly, they did not appeal to their master; their appeal was to Abigail. Her response was immediate:

> Abigail lost no time. She took two hundred loaves of bread, two skins of wine, five dressed sheep, five seahs of roasted grain, a hundred cakes of raisins, and two hundred cakes of pressed figs, and loaded them on donkeys. Then she told her servants, "Go on ahead; I'll follow you." But she did not tell her husband Nabal." (1 Samuel 25:18–19)

Abigail was intelligent, resourceful, and organized. It is no wonder she had the respect of her husband's servants. There is, however, something much more profound about this woman. David recognized it. "When Abigail saw David, she quickly got off her donkey and bowed down before David with her face to the ground. She fell at his feet and said: 'My lord, let the blame be on me alone. Please let your servant speak to you; hear what your servant has to say'" (1 Samuel 25:23–24).

After listening to Abigail, David exclaimed:

> Praise be to the LORD, the God of Israel, who has sent you today to meet me. May you be blessed for your good judgment and for keeping me from bloodshed this day and from avenging myself with my own hands. Otherwise, as surely as the LORD, the God of Israel, lives, who has kept me from harming you, if you had not come quickly to meet me, not one male belonging to Nabal would have been left alive by daybreak. (1 Samuel 25:32–34)

Abigail returned home. The next morning when her husband was sober she told him what had happened. "His heart failed him, and he became like a stone. About ten days later, the LORD struck Nabal and he died" (v. 37–38).

David now reacted quickly. "David sent word to Abigail, asking her to become his wife" (v. 39).

Abigail was an encourager to David. She "spurred him on to love and good deeds." She "inspired him to continue on his chosen course." Her incredible organizational skills to prepare such a large quantity of food, and her courage to take the risk of approaching David, are admirable. But I believe it was forgiveness that equipped her to be an encourager. The colossal barrier that prevents many people from being encouragers is unforgiveness. I am fascinated with Abigail because I believe her story shows us how to break through this barrier.

Abigail had apparently worked through this critical element of spiritual development. Remember, she was married to a surly (arrogant, irritably sullen and churlish in mood or manner, menacing or threatening in appearance) and mean man. She likely had to contend with neglect, insensitivity, verbal abuse,

---

The colossal barrier that prevents many people from being encouragers is unforgiveness.

---

and moodiness from him. There is no mention of children. The problem was not with Abigail for she and David later had a son. This makes me wonder if she suffered his rejection of her physically. I also wonder about her father, for in that culture marriages were arranged. How could a father give his daughter to a surly and mean man?

Abigail must have battled insecurity, fear, resentment, rejection, pride, anger, and a host of other emotions; yet she overcame these barriers. I am confident that she was not consumed with her situation. If she had been a woman wallowing in bitterness and self-pity, she would not have been so approachable. Remember, Nabal's servants had no hesitancy in going to her. Abigail's spirit was not bound by her predicament. She was not emotionally paralyzed. She had a freedom to relate to others and to act with precision and quickness in a crisis.

Restraining Bitterness and Resentment

It looks to me as if forgiveness ran deep in Abigail's character. Scripture tells us that she did not tell her husband she was going to take provisions to David. Some may think this was defiance on her part or that she did not demonstrate a submissive spirit. I beg to disagree. The man was in a drunken stupor. She told him, but she wisely waited until the next day when he was sober. Rather than defiance, I see protection. Consider her words to David: "Let the blame be on me alone."

Protection is a fruit of forgiveness.

Abigail could have done nothing, and David would have killed her husband. Then she would be rid of the man. But she demonstrated intense loyalty in defending him and assuming the blame for his actions. Her actions in his defense flowed from a forgiving spirit.

How could a woman forgive a man who had obviously inflicted such pain on her? I think the clue to her forgiving spirit is seen in her words to David: "Now since the Lord has kept you, my master, from bloodshed . . ." (v. 26).

The Hebrew name that Abigail uses to refer to God is *Yahweh*, His personal name. In this name He reveals Himself as the god of covenant faithfulness who has entered into a relationship with His people. He was not just an impersonal God to Abigail. He was Yahweh, and she had a personal relationship with Him.

Abigail gently reminds David that the Lord has kept him from bloodshed in the past. She knew that if David was restrained now, it would not be her charm that would restrain him. It would be God's grace. This makes me wonder if this woman had learned the power of God's grace to restrain the bitterness and resentment in her soul—

> Please forgive your servant's offense, for the LORD will certainly make a lasting dynasty for my master, because he fights the LORD'S battles. (v. 28)

Abigail somehow knew that David was the anointed of the Lord. Though her husband saw David as a renegade, Abigail knew better. God's sovereign plan was being carried out, and she

---

Abigail seems to have first-hand experience with the vanity of revenge.

---

challenged David not to be bogged down in insignificant pettiness but to get things in perspective. Had she coped with her situation by viewing it in light of the bigger picture of eternity?

> Let no wrongdoing be found in you as long as you live. Even though someone is pursuing you to take your life, the life of my master will be bound securely in the bundle of the living by the LORD your God. But the lives of your enemies he will hurl away as from the pocket of a sling. When the LORD has done for my master every good thing he promised concerning him and has appointed him leader over Israel, my master will not have on his conscience the staggering burden of needless bloodshed or of having avenged himself. (v. 28–31)

Abigail seems to have first-hand experience with the vanity of revenge. She must have learned the hollowness of focusing on present insults rather than rejoicing in the promises of God.

Abigail could talk about forgiveness with credibility. I suspect that she had to live a life of daily forgiveness to maintain her sanity and her faith. But her ability to forgive was entrenched in her relationship with Jehovah. She was a forgiven woman; thus she was freed to be a forgiving woman.

David married Abigail, and in the next chapter, we see that he regains his spiritual composure and once again magnanimously spares Saul's life. Oh, the influence of a godly woman!

It seems to me that there is compelling evidence that forgiveness freed and equipped Abigail to be an encourager.

We all have barriers in our lives. People have hurt us. Circumstances have defeated us. These things form barricades that obstruct our ability to relate to others unless they are demolished. Forgiveness is the only force powerful enough to level those barricades. This kind of thorough forgiveness is the result of grace. God's unending grace provides the power that is necessary to forgive.

Failure to forgive not only erects a barrier between us and the person who has offended us. Failure to forgive erects a barrier between us and God:

> And when you stand praying, if you hold anything against anyone, forgive him, so that your Father in heaven may forgive you your sins. (Mark 11:25)

Failure to forgive also forfeits our ability to encourage others. A woman who has not dealt with the hurts in her life and forgiven those who have offended her will have roots of bitterness and anger that will render her ineffective in entering into a nurturing relationship with a younger woman to encourage and equip her to live for God's glory. The warning in Hebrews is applicable here:

> See to it that no one misses the grace of God and that no bitter root grows up to cause trouble and defile many. (Hebrews 12:15)

Unless those roots are pulled out, they will show up when we are dealing with a woman who may be experiencing similar hurts and adversely affect the advice we give her—thus defiling her. Roots of bitterness due to past offenses defile present relationships. Refusal to forgive puts us under the domination of the person who has offended us, and that enslavement robs us of the freedom to have healthy relationships.

Forgiveness is perhaps the most powerful tool of the believer. Dr. Larry Crabb has said, "If we realize that forgiveness is the showcase of God's grace, then we will learn the joys of our new identity by devoting ourselves to worshipping God and serving others."[2]

The Fruit of Grace

The classic example of forgiveness is Stephen. When the mob became so furious over his sermon that they rushed at him, dragged him out of the city, and began stoning him, Stephen cried out, "Lord, do not hold this sin against them." We stand in such awe at this example that we often miss the most awesome part of this story. Before Stephen prayed that God would forgive his tormentors, he looked up and "saw the glory of God, and Jesus standing at the right hand of God" (Acts 7:55).

Stephen's ability to forgive was the direct result of his glimpse of the glory of God. His view of his offenders was obliterated by his view of God's glory. The vertical view gave him a totally different perspective of the horizontal view. But Stephen did have to look up. If he had kept his eyes on the stones zooming towards him, he would have missed that vertical view.

Forgiveness is the fruit of grace. As people who have experienced firsthand the glorious grace of God, we have the power to extend forgiveness even to our enemies. But we do have to look up. Sometimes we are so busy dodging the stones that we forget. That is when we need a spiritual mother to come alongside and help us. We need encouragement and support to raise our eyes heavenward.

A spiritual mother can't change the fact that a young woman's biological mother constantly criticizes her—but she can help that young woman see that her worth is in her identity as a daughter of the King and that she must forgive her mother though the mother may never change.

A spiritual mother can't change the fact that a woman's husband does not communicate love and appreciation—but she can pray with her that she will find her encouragement in Christ and be able to forgive her husband for this deficiency. She can encourage a young woman to trust God for this "desire of her heart" and to wait upon Him.

A spiritual mother can't change the fact that a woman did not get a deserved promotion in her law firm because of her involvement in pro-life rallies—but she can encourage her to see the big picture of God's plan and to forgive those who have discriminated against her.

Scores of women today have walls around them. Some of them have built walls to hide from the pain of incest, rape, rejection, or ridicule. Some have built walls to hide from the sorrow of divorce or rebellious children. Some have built walls to hide from the pain of their own actions such as an abortion or unfaithfulness. Even though the walls are their protection against painful memories, these walls obstruct healthy relationships. These women need spiritual mothers who will encourage and equip them to forgive.

To nurture something means to promote its growth and development. Probably nothing will stifle spiritual growth and development as much as an unforgiving spirit, and nothing will stimulate growth and development as much as forgiveness.

Only forgivers can teach forgiveness with the credibility that is necessary to be believable. This presupposes that offenses have occurred. Unforgiveness is costly, but we must acknowledge that it is also costly to forgive. Forgiveness means releasing—giving up—turning loose. But forgiveness has a positive pay-back; unforgiveness keeps on costing.

We have some incredible contemporary female role models of forgiveness.

In *The Hiding Place*, Corrie ten Boom tells of her experiences in a Nazi concentration camp. Her sister Betsie's dying words burned in her heart: "We must go everywhere. We must tell people that no pit is so deep that He is not deeper still. They will believe us, because we were here."[3]

These words compelled Corrie to fulfill Betsie's dream of a home where people could heal from the trauma of imprisonment:

> Hundreds of people arrived at the beautiful home in Bloemendaal. Silent or endlessly relating their losses, withdrawn or fiercely aggressive, every one was a damaged human being. Not all had been in concentration camps; some had spent two, three, even four years hidden in attic rooms and back closets here in Holland. . . . for all these people alike, the key to healing turned out to be the same. Each had a hurt he had to forgive: the neighbor who had reported him, the brutal guard, the sadistic soldier.[4]

And then Corrie tells of her most difficult forgiveness-encounter:

> It was at a church service in Munich that I saw him, the former S.S. man who had stood guard at the shower room door in the processing center at Ravensbruck. He was the first of our actual jailers that I had seen since that time. And suddenly it was all there—the roomful of mocking men, the heaps of clothing, Betsie's pain-blanched face.
>
> He came up to me as the church was emptying, beaming and bowing. "How grateful I am for your message, *Fraulein*," he said. "To think that, as you say, He has washed my sins away!"
>
> His hand was thrust out to shake mine. And I, who had preached so often to the people in Bloemendaal the need to forgive, kept my hand at my side.
>
> Even as the angry vengeful thoughts boiled through me, I saw the sin of them. Jesus Christ had died for this man; was I going to ask for more? Lord Jesus, I prayed, forgive me and help me to forgive him.
>
> I tried to smile, I struggled to raise my hand. I could not. I felt nothing, not the slightest spark of warmth or charity. And so again I breathed a silent prayer. Jesus, I cannot forgive him. Give me Your forgiveness.
>
> As I took his hand the most incredible thing happened. From my shoulder along my arm and through my hand a current seemed to pass from me to him, while into my heart sprang a love for this stranger that almost overwhelmed me.

And so I discovered that it is not on our forgiveness any more than on our goodness that the world's healing hinges, but on His. When He tells us to love our enemies, He gives, along with the command, the love itself.[5]

There is also the remarkable story of the five missionaries who were killed by the Auca Indians. In the foreword to *The Savage My Kinsman* by Elisabeth Elliot, Cornell Capa writes:

The widows believed that their husbands' death was not the meaningless tragedy it appeared to many. No thoughts of revenge crossed their minds; on the contrary, they felt with an increased sense of urgency the need to bring their message of love and redemption to the Aucas.[6]

This book is the story of Elisabeth Elliot's years living among the Indians who killed her husband and sharing Christ with them.

Gail MacDonald is another believable woman on the topic of forgiveness. Her wise words on this topic have the ring of one who has walked the path of forgiveness. In her book *Keep Climbing*, she writes:

Consider one woman who is deeply hurt by the failure of another and chooses not to forgive. In so doing, she effectively nails herself to that event and time and makes her climb a difficult one. Another woman, however, knows a similar betrayal and chooses to manage the pain and hurt by giving mercy and forgiving grace. She not only steadily moves beyond the event to further growth but gains a bit more strength and resilience to become an even more forgiving person in the future. One act of forgiveness usually begets another.

Forgiveness—discarding the weight of anger and resentment—is of particular interest to me. I know what it's like to face the challenge of forgiveness, and I am in touch with a significant number of women who have faced it, too. All of this has taught me that being a forgiving person may be one of the most important matters a modern Christian woman can pursue. . . .

> Forgiveness is more often a life-style of grace than a one-time act. We have fooled ourselves if we think that the resolve to forgive someone who has hurt us can be wrapped up in an overnight decision. That's an unreal expectation and an inhuman pressure to put upon ourselves.[7]

These women, like Abigail, penetrated the barrier of unforgiveness. Through forgiveness, their inner wounds were healed, their service in the kingdom was expanded, and they became engaging encouragers to countless numbers of God's children.

Women who have had the opportunity to extend forgiveness have the privilege and the responsibility to teach the art of forgiveness. The question is, what are we going to do with our hurts? Are we going to allow them to immobilize us, or will we turn them into valuable resources to encourage and equip others to forgive? Whether we use our hurts in negative, destructive ways or in positive, building ways depends on whether or not we forgive.

Forgiveness does not necessarily mean reconciliation. Often women truly forgive, but because there is no reconciliation with the one who has hurt them they labor under false guilt that they have not done everything they should. Reconciliation requires both repentance and forgiveness. There is a duel responsibility on the part of the offender and the offended. We cannot control the repentance of the one who has hurt us. We can only forgive. Our forgiveness may or may not bring about reconciliation, but it will free us to have a right relationship with God and with others.

The woman who has forgiven will have an alertness to the feelings and circumstances of others. This heightened sensitivity will cause her to be a woman of action. It will be intrinsic to her character to nurture and encourage others. This was true of Abigail, and she is described as a beautiful woman.

Whether or not Abigail had external beauty is irrelevant. I just do not think that external beauty is what God is telling us about this woman. When beauty is exalted in Scripture it is

---

**Our forgiveness may or may not
bring about reconciliation, but it
will free us to have a right
relationship with God
and with others.**

---

usually in connection with far more grand things than physical
form and features.

> Your beauty should not come from outward adornment such
> as braided hair and the wearing of gold jewelry and fine
> clothes. Instead, it should be that of your inner self, the un-
> fading beauty of a gentle and quiet spirit, which is of great
> worth in God's sight. For this is the way the holy women of
> the past who put their hope in God used to make themselves
> beautiful. (1 Peter 3:3–5)

What was Abigail's beauty secret? I think it was her forgiving spirit. As forgiven people, we really have no alternative but
to be forgivers:

> You are forgiving and good, O LORD . . . (Psalm 86:5)

> The LORD our God is merciful and forgiving, even though we
> have rebelled against him . . . (Daniel 9:9)

> If we confess our sins, he is faithful and just and will forgive us
> our sins and purify us from all unrighteousness. (1 John 1:9)

> Be kind and compassionate to one another, forgiving each
> other, just as in Christ God forgave you. (Ephesians 4:32)

 za   za   za

A Spiritual Mothering Challenge

1. Open with prayer.

   a. Meditate on Nehemiah 9:17.

   b. Reflect on the truth that you are a forgiven person. Then before God, ask yourself if you are a forgiving person. Ask Him to show you any root of anger or bitterness that may be hindering your relationship with Him, your relationship with others, and your ability to train others in the art of forgiveness. Determine to use every offense in your life for good.

   c. If there is anyone you are having difficulty forgiving, make a list of what it will cost you to forgive and what it will cost you not to forgive. Then, by God's grace, forgive.

2. Use the energy produced by forgiveness to reach out to a hurting woman. Write her a note, take her a meal, or invite her to lunch.

Mariam's Story

Barren! I don't care for that word much. It is so hard, cold, and final. In my case, it even hurts to say it.

After nine years of trying to have children, undergoing exhaustive, expensive tests and painful surgical procedures, I must now accept that I am infertile—in that graphic King James language: barren.

I have been blessed with opportunities most people would envy. I have worked in the United States Senate, at the White House and as a deputy assistant secretary for the largest federal agency in government. But much of that time, my mind focused more on getting pregnant and getting out of there rather than seizing the opportunities God gave me. You see, the plans I had for my life were career, marriage, and motherhood by age thirty. His plans were different.

The tears have been many; the pain indescribable. There is no doubt in my mind that God loves me, that His plans for my life are perfect, and His loving and sovereign hands enfold me. That doesn't mean, though, that it still doesn't hurt. The wonderful blessing in all this is what God is doing with that hurt in my life.

His answers began with questions as I played the "maybe next month" game. Questions like "What are you doing while you wait?" "How are you exercising the spiritual stewardship of each new day that I give you?" and the most persistent of all: "Why do you really want to be a mother?" I had lots of answers for that one ranging from the noble to self-serving.

More answers came after hearing a talk given by Elisabeth Elliot. I have always admired her no-nonsense approach to life, and she began to challenge us to understand God's call to believers to disciple others. When she began to explain the scope of what discipleship meant, it was as though she was speaking directly to me! I don't have to wait to physically birth a child in order to teach, to love or to nurture someone. I don't have to wait to show others how to make a difference for Jesus in this world. I can be a mother *now*. We are commanded to be spiritual disciplers, spiritual mothers. God gives us the passion and desire to love and teach. We have to get rid of the preconceived parameters of what "mothering" means.

Do I still wrestle with my lot as an infertile woman? Yes. Do I still cry? Yes. Can I still experience joy in life because of this? Without a doubt! I am now learning to appreciate the words of Paul and Isaiah: "Be glad, O barren woman, who bears no children; break forth and cry aloud, you who have no labor pains; because more are the children of the desolate woman than of her who has a husband" (Isaiah 54:1, Galatians 4:27).

Mariam Bell
Washington, D. C.

11

COMFORT
THE COMFORTLESS

As a mother comforts her child, so will I comfort you.
Isaiah 66:13

I nvolvement in someone's pain gives a dimension to a relationship that nothing else is able to do. So often people suffer alone because we lack the comforting skills that will give us
the confidence to be comforters. The words of David pierce our
hearts:

> Scorn has broken my heart and has left me helpless; I looked
> for sympathy, but there was none, for comforters, but I found
> none. (Psalm 69:20)

Many broken-hearted women feel helpless. They sit on the
pew next to us, but they suffer in silence because they are afraid
we will reject them if we know about the abortion or the son
who is in jail or the daughter who is pregnant or the husband
who is an alcoholic. Women have told me that they seek out
support groups away from their churches because they can't bear
to risk exposing their pain inside their churches.

Other women's hurting hearts leave them feeling helpless
because they think it is wrong to feel pain. These women have
somehow gotten the idea that Christians should not suffer depression or fear or grief. They are ashamed to admit their pain.

In both kinds of situations, we as individuals and collectively
as the church must examine the message we are communicating,

the atmosphere we are creating, and the skills we are developing. Are we comforting others as part of our ministry of encouragement?

The Message of Comfort

The message of comfort that we communicate will depend on our perspective of our own pain. We will not have a Biblical message of comfort until we have learned how to decipher our own hurts. Paul gives us great insight to the ministry of comfort in his letter to the church in Corinth. He begins his explanation of suffering in a strange way. He begins with a call to praise. The incongruity of praise and pain is senseless until we understand the purpose of our pain:

> Praise be to the God and Father of our Lord Jesus Christ, the Father of compassion and the God of all comfort, who comforts us in all our troubles, so that we can comfort those in any trouble with the comfort we ourselves have received from God. (2 Corinthians 1:3–4)

Once again we are confronted with one of those inclusive words—*all* leaves nothing out. The God of *all* comfort comforts us in *all* of our troubles. Nothing is outside the range of His ability to comfort us. This comfort is so compelling that it not only gives us relief, it also equips us to comfort others. So our pain has purpose. Without pain we would not experience God's comfort. Without experiencing God's comfort we are not equipped to comfort others. Now of course this makes no sense to the self-centered approach to life which has no concern about comforting others. However, it makes perfect sense to the servant whose life-purpose is God's glory. It makes perfect sense to the follower and imitator of the One who suffered in our place.

This passage goes on to address the degree of our suffering. Paul tells his Corinthian friends that he wants them to understand why the hardships he suffered were so brutal.

We were under great pressure, far beyond our ability to endure, so that we despaired even of life. Indeed, in our hearts we felt the sentence of death. But this happened that we might not rely on ourselves but on God, who raises the dead. (2 Corinthians 1:8–9)

The pressure was beyond his ability to endure—but this happened so that he would not rely on himself but on God. This profound perspective on suffering is absolutely essential if we are going to glorify God through our suffering and if we are going to encourage and equip others to glorify Him when they suffer. Our tendency to self-sufficiency can only be overcome

---

Our tendency to self-sufficiency can only be overcome when our situation is beyond our sufficiency.

---

when our situation is beyond our sufficiency. Only then will we learn experientially the sufficiency of Christ. And when we learn that, we have a message of comfort that is real. As long as my message is, "I did it; you can too," I will be a great discomfort to a hurting person. When I have been under pressure beyond my internal resources to handle and have learned how to rely on God, then I have a message of comfort. Then I can say with credibility:

He has delivered us from such a deadly peril, and he will deliver us. On him we have set our hope that he will continue to deliver us . . . (2 Corinthians 1:10)

The Atmosphere of Comfort

We need to formulate a Biblical message of comfort, and we also need to create an atmosphere where this message can be heard. We can learn volumes about creating an atmosphere

where others will be comforted from the women who followed
Jesus to the cross.

> Some women were watching from a distance. . . .
> In Galilee these women had followed him and cared for
> his needs. . . .
> Very early on the first day of the week, just after sunrise, they
> were on their way to the tomb. (Mark 15:40–41, 16:2)

How comforting the presence of these women must have been
to Jesus as He looked down from the cross. These women, who
had cared for His needs, did not desert Him when things got
tough. They were not too embarrassed by the shame of the cru-
cifixion to show up. Their pride was not bruised because the
One they had followed and invested in ended up on a cross
instead of in the king's palace. They did not turn away in fear
or disgust, nor did they become hysterical. There was nothing
they could do to change or "fix" the situation—but they were
there.

These women stayed to the end. They followed to see
where the body was laid. And then on the first day of the week,
they were on their way to the tomb. Even after witnessing the
horror of that event, they were not too overcome with emotional and physical fatigue to do what remained to be done.
There was kingdom service to render, and they were on their
way to do it. They were there. And by being there, one of them
was the first person to see the resurrected Lord!

Caring enough to "be there" communicates loving involvement in another's pain. Hurting people require enormous energy just to survive. We can be a further drain on their energies
through insensitive remarks or neglect, or we can provide an
atmosphere of love that makes it easier for them to experience
God's comfort.

I blush to think how often I have done nothing because I
didn't know what to do. If the crisis is "delicate," I am especially unsure of myself. I say nothing to the woman who is
going through a divorce or to the woman whose unmarried
daughter is pregnant because I don't want to embarrass her. My

hurting sister interprets my silence as rejection, and she hurts even more. I may be praying for her daily, but if I don't tell her, she feels isolated and says with David, "I looked for sympathy . . . for comforters . . . but found none." By not being there for her, I do not provide a safe environment for her wounds to heal.

By involving ourselves in another person's pain, we can help them experience God's comfort. An atmosphere of love will facilitate healing for wounded people. All of us cannot and

---

Caring enough to "be there" communicates loving involvement in another's pain.

---

should not be counselors. Often professional counselling is needed, and we can do great harm by attempting to do more than we are equipped to do. Yet we can all be comforters—we can be there for the hurting person, and we can share with them the comfort we have received from God.

But how do we communicate our message of comfort? How do we create an atmosphere of comfort? We need to develop comforting skills.

Developing Comforting Skills

Perhaps the following "formula" will help you develop comforting skills that will give you the confidence to reach out to women who are hurting.

Study. Study the hurting person to determine what she needs. People react to situations differently and their needs are different. I have two daughters whose reaction to emotional pain is entirely different. One immediately wants to hear words, say words, and feel someone touching her. The other wants to be alone and process things before she speaks or listens. One reaction is not better; they are just different. But I had to study my girls to learn this. I had to learn that everyone does not react as I do and that they may not want to be comforted the same way I want to be comforted. Sometimes we need to ask the person in pain what she needs from us. The important thing is to communicate that we want to help but that we need to know how.

Not only do different people react differently to pain, but various situations require different responses. Someone who has been through a similar experience can help us. The widow who cared for her husband during his illness can tell us what a women in a similar situation needs. The woman who has been through a divorce knows practical things that are needed in this situation. Women need to pool their knowledge and their energies to provide comfort to hurting sisters.

Speak. This does not necessarily mean a verbal message, but it does mean that we should do something. Silence is not silent, and hurting people are terrible interpreters. They hear through filters of pain, and they will almost always misinterpret our silence. Written or spoken words or a hug tells the person that you care. A note that simply says, "I care about you, and I am praying for you" will communicate your concern.

Our words can be a help or a hindrance in the healing process. The following practical ideas were gathered from conversations with many women who were willing to use their experiences to teach others how to comfort. Here are their responses to my question, "Tell me how another woman comforted you when you went through your particular experience."

I was comforted when . . .

- A woman who had been through a divorce came to my home after my husband left me. She hugged me, cried with me, and prayed for me. She assured me that God would never leave or forsake me.

- A friend sent me a card each month for a year following my husband's death.

- A friend remembered that Mother's Day was difficult for me, because I desperately wanted to be a mother. She simply hugged me and said, "I love you."

- A friend placed value on my experience of pain by asking, "Will you share with me what God has taught you so that I can minister to others going through the same thing?"

- An older woman told me that I had been a good mother, and she was confident God would do a work of grace in my child. She assured me that it was not my fault that my teenager had been arrested and that God would work even that out for His glory.

- An older woman at church told me that she would pray daily for my unbelieving husband and that she was proud of me for bringing the children to church.

- The women in my church took turns staying with me after I was raped. They read Scripture to me, prayed with me, and never left me alone until I felt I was ready. Over and over they told me that I was not to blame until finally I began to believe it.

- During my chemotherapy treatments, the women in my church brought meals every day, cleaned my house once a week, and told me they wanted me to use all my energy to get well.

- A woman wrote me a note and shared several Scripture verses of promise and hope.

- My husband was unemployed, and an older woman who had been through this called every week to encourage me not to lose confidence in my husband. She helped me understand what he was going through. She also frequently brought over a meal that was enough to last for several days!

- After the death of my child, a friend called every morning for weeks (I forget how many!). The conversations were short unless I wanted to talk. One day, as I shared how God had comforted me through His Word, she said, "What you have just said tells me that you are going to be all right. I won't be calling you every morning from now on because you don't need for me to do that. But when you do need me, just call." Realizing that she had confidence in me was such an encouragement.

I also asked women what had happened that was hurtful to them during their time of suffering—what things hindered their healing process. It is just as important for us to know what not to do as it is to know what to do.

I was *not* comforted when . . .

- I had a miscarriage and someone said, "You're young, you can try again." That wasn't the issue. My heart was breaking over the child that had died.

- People visited for long periods of time when I was emotionally and physically drained from the trauma of my situation.

- My teenage daughter was pregnant, and no one said anything.

- My friend told me it was partly my fault that my son was on drugs. She said that if I had not had the part-time job, it wouldn't have happened.

Oh, that we would remember: "Pleasant words are a honeycomb; sweet to the soul and healing to the bones" (Proverbs 16:24).

Stick. Often a hurting person needs comfort long-term. Frequently widows have shared how there were many friends around until the funeral. But after the funeral "they looked for comforters but found none." Of course we can't all stick by every person who is going through a painful situation, but we should be sensitive to the fact that continued comfort is needed. Perhaps several friends can take a day a week to call the new widow. Or several families can plan together to be sure she has an invitation to lunch after church on Sundays.

Healing takes time. A deep wound takes a long time to heal. We must be patient with and sensitive to the woman who is healing. This does not mean that we become an enabler and

---

Healing takes time. A deep wound takes a long time to heal. We must be patient with and sensitive to the woman who is healing.

---

allow her to become dependent on us. It does mean that we are an encourager, equipping her to depend on God. Reaching out and touching the life of a woman in pain will encourage her. It will also equip her to reach out to someone else.

Called to be Comforters

In *A Chance to Die*, Elisabeth Elliot tells of Amy Carmichael's "inescapable calling" to the mission field. "It was on that snowy Wednesday evening that the categorical imperative came, not just once but again and again: *Go ye*."[1]

There were many reasons not to go. She had been caring for an elderly man, Mr. Wilson, and knew it would break his heart for her to leave. She also felt a responsibility for her mother. The calling was clear, but the struggle was painful. Amy offered herself to Hudson Taylor's China Inland Mission and Mr. Wilson took her to London, to the home of Miss Soltau, who was in charge of women candidates.

> Wilson returned home. That night Amy was overcome with sorrow. . . . She stood by the window of her little bedroom, tortured with thoughts of his desolation. Miss Soltau came and stood beside her:
> The window had been open, and the little white dressing-table cover was powdered with smuts. As a tortured heart

does always notice trifles, so I noticed those smuts. The words broke from me, "They say that if I leave him he will die. Even so am I right to go?" "Yes," was Miss Soltau's answer, "I think even so, you are right to go."

It was a tremendous answer. She must have added something about trusting our Father to deal tenderly with His servant who had truly given me to Him, though his heart still clung to me. But all I remember of the next few minutes is that with her arms around me I entered into peace. Often, through the many years that have passed since that night, I have been helped by the memory of her courage in the ways of God to strengthen a younger soul who was being torn as I was then.[2]

God intends for us to comfort one another. Paul wrote to the people in Corinth:

> For when we came into Macedonia, this body of ours had no rest, but we were harassed at every turn—conflicts on the outside, fears within. But God, who comforts the downcast, comforted us by the coming of Titus, and not only by his coming but also by the comfort you had given him. He told us about your longing for me, you deep sorrow, your ardent concern for me, so that my joy was greater than ever. (2 Corinthians 7:5–7)

Titus and the Corinthian Christians were God's instruments of comfort for Paul. The presence of Titus and the knowledge that the Corinthian church cared gave joy to Paul's weary, troubled soul.

Perhaps you are the person who is hurting right now and you have to say with David, "I looked for comforters but found none . . ." If so, it will be easy for you to be your own hindrance to healing if you use others' neglect to excuse self-pity. Even if there are no comforters, you must do what David did. He looked for comforters, but there were none. So he did the right thing anyway. He praised God.

> I am in pain and distress; may your salvation, O God, protect me. I will praise God's name in song and glorify him with

thanksgiving. This will please the LORD more than an ox, more than a bull with its horns and hoofs. (Psalm 69:29–31)

I am saddened if you are suffering alone, but I urge you to avail yourself of the sufficiency of the God of *all* comfort who can comfort you in *all* your troubles. Use your alone time to drink deeply of His Word and to spend much time in prayer. And then turn your trouble into a treasure by using what you learn about Him to be a comforter to others.

Hurting times are prime times to encourage and equip a younger woman to glorify God. But we can only do this through the ministry of comfort. Our presence must be a safety zone for hurting people. Our churches must be safe places not only for those with mentionable hurts but also for those with unmentionable hurts. We must make a conscious effort to incorporate comfort into our personal and collective ministries.

Women have a capacity for comfort and an inclination for action which are powerful resources in our churches. When women's nurturing instincts are mobilized, the ministry of comfort in a church is energized. Comfort creates the context in which a woman can be encouraged and equipped to use her pain for God's glory. Let us determine that no woman among us will have to say, "I looked for comforters but found none."

᷁᷁᷁᷁᷁᷁᷁᷁ ᷁᷁᷁᷁᷁᷁᷁᷁ ᷁᷁᷁᷁᷁᷁᷁᷁

A Spiritual Mothering Challenge

1. Begin with prayer.

   a. Meditate on Psalm 23:4.

   b. Evaluate your perspective of your own times of suffering. Have you learned to find your comfort in God and to use times of pain for His glory? Have you been equipped to comfort others by what you have learned about God's sufficiency? Praise Him! And turn that praise into practice by reaching out to comfort someone else with the comfort you have received from Him.

2. Pray that God will show you a woman who needs comfort. Ask Him to put her next to you at church on Sunday—or to burden you to call her—or to nudge you to take a meal to her.

Penny's Story

I was all of seventeen when I first encountered Carolyn. I found her perched in her bedroom, sewing, and answering all the questions and interruptions that four children can conceive. A Southern lady, she was pretty and small, yet her world revolved around her as if she were command central. Although we had just met, she managed to make me feel like the most important guest she had seen in months. That afternoon she asked me questions and responded to me as if I were full of wisdom. I was shocked to learn that an adult cared to find out what a teenager knew. While biting off threads and serving tea, she asked my opinion about everything. I left her house realizing I *had* opinions, and someone cared to hear them. I had no idea that afternoon the role this lady would play in my life.

Over six years later, when I was newly married and lonely in an unfamiliar city, God brought our lives together again. Carolyn used her eyes to see a young woman with potential. Our relationship grew as a result of her ordinary skills: talking to me after church, calling me up to see how I was adjusting to married life, and encouraging me to attend specific functions at our church. Simply put, I felt my presence mattered to her.

I spent many days at her house sitting at her counter while she prepared dinner or cleaned up the mess a family of six leaves behind. She taught me budgeting, how to present a tuna sandwich as if it were gourmet cuisine, and how to maintain a calm demeanor while the phone rang and someone unexpectedly pulled into the driveway. I saw her at her best and sometimes as her edges unraveled. She was no superwoman, just a godly one, ever ready to admit weakness and sin. She allowed me to see her life and taught me to enjoy the benefits of being forgiven by God. I soaked in everything she offered, and she absorbed what I had to offer in areas she was willing to explore.

Every Friday we had lunch together. Apart from the significance of having specific time with her, I learned the importance of praying with a friend. Over the course of time, she would foster and encourage my thinking. On occasions, she would listen to my inexperienced thinking with loving ears and allow me to see the folly of my own conclusions. When necessary, she told me carefully and lovingly where and why I was wrong. My skills as a leader were carefully being supervised and evaluated yet in an unassuming way.

John and I began to think of going to seminary in Philadelphia with the goal of ministering together. I had sensed in me a burning desire to listen to others with my heart, and Carolyn suggested that I pursue graduate work in the field of counseling. Her love for me had produced a woman eager to serve others with the gifts God had given me.

Although Carolyn and I are separated by distance, we maintain our love for each other by phone calls and visits. My life is full of parenting, counseling, housekeeping, and speaking to groups of women. The fruit of my life grows as a direct result of God's grace and a woman committed to loving me well.

Penny Nelson Freeman
Philadelphia, Pennsylvania

12

STAYING . . . AND SEPARATING

Mary stayed with Elizabeth for
about three months and then returned home.

Luke 1:56

T he balance between staying and separating is tricky. It takes energy to stay in a relationship and to encourage and equip long-term. It takes confidence on the part of both women to turn loose and separate. There is no easy formula to know when to do which thing. But there are some Biblical principles that can guide us.

Energy to Stay

Investing in a younger woman in order to encourage and equip her to live for God's glory requires enormous energy. Motivation and renewal are key factors in our spiritual energy level.

I see three levels of motivation for the Christian. All are important and Biblical, but only the third level will enable us to tenaciously stick with another person.

The first level is love for the other person. The account of Jesus serving His disciples by washing their feet begins by saying, "Having loved his own who were in the world, he now showed them the full extent of his love" (John 13:1). Love produced service. Energy is power in action. The power of my love for others should and does energize me to serve them. But if I am really honest, I must admit that sometimes my love does not produce sufficient energy to stick with that woman who is not progressing as quickly as I think she should or with that woman who is just not pleasant to deal with. Then I must move to the second level of motivation.

The second level is love for Jesus. This is part of what Jesus was teaching Peter when, after the resurrection, He asked, "Simon, son of John, do you truly love me?" Three times Jesus asked the question, and three times Peter replied "Lord, you know that I love you." Jesus' response was, "Feed my lambs. . . . Take care of my sheep. . . . Feed my sheep" (John 21:15–17). I know that there are many lessons in this passage, but one unmistakable lesson is that if I love Jesus, I will feed and take care of His lambs.

I have no personal experience with sheep, but I understand that they are not particularly pleasant creatures. They are often smelly, stubborn, and lazy—not unlike some people we must deal with! Yet we are to feed and care for them because we love Jesus. I wish I could say that my love for my Lord supplies the necessary energy for the task. Often it does, but often it does not. Just as my love for others is whimsical, I must confess that my love for Jesus is not as steadfast as it should be. When neither my love for others nor my love for Jesus furnishes the vitality that is needed to feed and care for the lambs, there is yet another level of motivation that never runs dry.

The first two levels of motivation are within myself and therefore not always reliable. The third level of motivation is outside myself and never changes. The Apostle Paul expresses it for us: "For Christ's love compels us" (2 Corinthians 5:14). Paul is not saying that his love for Christ compels him: He was under no illusions about the reliability of his internal motivation. Remember this is the man who said, "I know that nothing good lives in me, that is, in my sinful nature. For I have the desire to do what is good, but I cannot carry it out. For what I do is not the good I want to do; no, the evil I do not want to do—this I keep on doing. . . . What a wretched man I am!

Who will rescue me from this body of death? Thanks be to God—through Jesus Christ our Lord!" (Romans 7:18–19, 24–25).

"For Christ's love compels us." The sheep are sometimes dirty. Sometimes they are difficult. Not all the sheep are lovable, and too often I don't love them enough to feed and care for them. And what's worse, my love for Jesus is sometimes in short supply. But when I stand back and reflect on His unconditional, unchanging love for me, I am energized. Renewal begins when I reach down to this third level of motivation. Renewal continues as I fellowship with Him in prayer and study of His Word. Through worship my energy is replenished.

Jesus calls us to feed and care for His sheep, but even as we go about that task, He feeds and cares for us.

> The Lord is my shepherd, I shall lack nothing. He makes me lie down in green pastures, he leads me beside quiet waters, he restores my soul. (Psalm 23:1–3)

Confidence to Separate

The time came when Mary had to return to Nazareth. Some commentators say that Joseph may not have known about

---

When I stand back and reflect on His unconditional, unchanging love for me, I am energized.

Mary's pregnancy until she returned. By that time it would have been obvious. Returning may have meant confronting Joseph. It surely meant confronting everyone else in town. It would have been so much easier to stay in the safety of Elizabeth's home. Still it was time to separate.

Mary and Elizabeth had three very intimate months together. It took confidence for Mary to leave, and I think it took confidence for Elizabeth to let her go. Mary must have looked so fragile as she walked away from Elizabeth's home. I wonder how long Elizabeth stood at the door watching her. I wonder how many times Mary came back for one more reassuring hug. I wonder how hard Elizabeth had to bite her tongue to keep from telling Mary to come back and stay a while longer.

I think I know something of what each woman felt, but at this point in my life, I am trying to learn from Elizabeth. Being a spiritual mother means instilling Christ-confidence in a young woman so that she can leave me and face the world. This is scary.

Two weeks before I began writing this book some single college/career women asked if we could get together to talk about how they could live for Jesus. Our weekly "girl talk" sessions have been an affirmation from the Lord about the importance of older women training younger women. One night I asked them why they sought out an older woman. I am old enough to be their biological mother: in fact, my youngest daughter is part of the group. They mentioned several things, but my daughter, Laurin, summed it up when she said, "We only see what is happening right now—you can see what is coming. You can help us see the consequences of our choices ahead of time."

Our times together this summer have been precious. I have seen so much growth in these young women. I have rejoiced when they have made some good choices. I have agonized when I knew they were close to making some wrong choices. Summer will soon be over, and some of them will be returning to college—yet they look so fragile to me. Will they continue to make right choices without our sessions together? Just this morning I began praying Paul's prayer for the Colossians for these young women:

> . . . asking God to fill you with the knowledge of his will through all spiritual wisdom and understanding . . . in order that you may live a life worthy of the Lord and may please him in every way: bearing fruit in every good work, growing in the knowledge of God, being strengthened with all power

---

Being a spiritual mother means instilling Christ-confidence in a young woman so that she can leave me and face the world.

---

according to his glorious might so that you may have great endurance and patience. (Colossians 1:9–11)

But I still felt fearful about "turning loose" until the Lord gave me confidence through His Word. I was reading the passage in Romans dealing with Christian liberty, when the verses spoke to my situation with these young women:

Accept him whose faith is weak. . . . Who are you to judge someone else's servant? To his own master he stands or falls. And he will stand, for the Lord is able to make him stand. (Romans 14:1, 4)

Confidence welled up in me—not confidence in "my girls" but in the truth that they belong to *Him* and that *He is able to make them stand.*

Now I can release them with confidence. And I must give them confidence to leave. This is a mark of a good teacher; it characterizes the ministry Jesus had with His students. Jesus called the disciples to be "with him" that they might become "like him." After He left them, some of them were called before the "rulers and elders and scribes . . . and Annas the high priest was there, and Caiaphas and John and Alexander, and all who were of high-priestly descent . . ." (Acts 4:5–6). This could have been an intimidating experience for these former fishermen. But the religious leaders' reaction to the defense of these men is revealing:

Now as they observed the confidence of Peter and John, and understood that they were uneducated and untrained men, they were marveling, and began to recognize them as having been with Jesus. (Acts 4:13, NASB)

The distinguishing characteristic of the students of Jesus was confidence! Being with Jesus produced this confidence. This was not self-confidence in their own abilities. They possessed a Christ-confidence in His ability to keep them from falling and to present them before His glorious presence without fault and with great joy (Jude 24).

A Change in Relationship

I get the feeling that Elizabeth poured this kind of confidence into Mary. After being with Elizabeth for three months, Mary returned to Nazareth and assumed the responsibility she had been given.

Separation does not mean the end of the relationship, but it does mean a change in the relationship. Knowing when and how to make this change and to release a biological or spiritual daughter to adulthood takes much prayer.

U. S. News and World Report recorded an interesting interview with Terri Apter, author of *Altered Loves*, a study of mothers and daughters:

> In my study, I found that what an adolescent girl is trying to do is not to separate but to renegotiate the relationship with her mother. She doesn't want to lose her mother's love, but she wants to work very hard to establish a new balance, whereby the mother's view is not stronger than her own. Though daughters did talk about separating from their mothers, much more frequent were complaints about "what my mother understands, what my mother will listen to." The daughters were criticizing their mothers' views of them. There just wasn't separation going on.

When asked if girls are different from boys in this way she responded:

> My work shows that there is more uniformity among girls than there is among boys. Take almost any girl, and she's going to care a great deal about what her mother thinks, and

she's going to want to express herself to her mother and try to get her mother to acknowledge her. My impression from others' work is that while some boys care very much what one parent or the other thinks, others are just not sensitive in that way. They're not hurt by other people's reactions, and they don't seek their parents' understanding or confirmation.[1]

Some helpful insights here apply to our biological and spiritual daughters. The time comes when they are ready to "separate." It seems to me that it is important for the mother to recognize this even before the daughter does and to encourage it. If the daughter has to initiate it, and if the mother resists it,

---

Often biological mothers and daughters experience conflict in planning the daughter's wedding. They attribute it to the "pressure" of the wedding. I think it's more than that. Is it possible that what is really happening is that the daughter is trying to separate and the mother is resisting?

---

there is conflict. If the mother encourages and supports it, and if she gives her understanding and approval, the relationship actually becomes stronger. Separation, if done correctly, strengthens rather than weakens the relationship. Separation means releasing the daughter to adulthood and relating to her as an adult. What does this mean practically? How do we push this principle out into practice?

Often biological mothers and daughters experience conflict in planning the daughter's wedding. They attribute it to the "pressure" of the wedding. I think it's more than that. Is it possible that what is really happening is that the daughter is trying to separate and the mother is resisting? The daughter is trying to "leave and cleave," and the mother is terrified of losing her baby. When the daughter asks "Mom, which wedding dress (apartment, dishes, etc.) do you think I should get?" is it really an obligatory question? Perhaps what she wants is not her mother's advice but rather her approval to be an adult. She needs to know that her mother thinks she is capable of making good decisions. It is a wise mother who gently backs out of the picture and makes room for her daughter to separate emotionally. A wise mother lovingly tells the daughter that it is her wedding or her dishes, and it should be what she wants. The daughter wants to please the mother, but this is a wonderful opportunity for a mother to do much more than express an opinion on a dress or dishes. This is an opportunity to demonstrate confidence in a daughter. This "renegotiating" actually makes the relationship stronger.

Many years ago, as a young mother, I was greatly blessed and influenced by a single parent in our church. Hazel had a beautiful relationship with her daughter Claire. Throughout Claire's senior year in high school I wondered how Hazel would handle it when Claire went away to college. As I watched and listened to this wise woman, I began to understand why she had such a strong relationship with her daughter. She told me how empty and quiet the house was now that Claire was gone, but with a twinkle in her eyes she said, "But Claire will never know that. In fact, when I write her I sometimes tell her that I only have time for a short note. I do not want Claire to think that I am sitting here alone. I want her to know that my life will go on, and I want her to have the freedom to go on with her life."

I have appreciated this same attitude in my own mother. After my dad died, Mamma quickly re-focused her life. She was determined not to shift her dependence to her children and "cling" to us. This spunky seventy-five-year old lady took cooking and sewing classes, began going to the gym, widened her circle of friends, and reached out to help other widows. She has gained a new level of respect from her children and grandchildren.

When a spiritual daughter asks whether or not she should make a particular career choice or whether she should accept the responsibility of coordinating the women's ministry visitation program, it may be time to encourage her to make this decision on her own. It is important to let her know that you believe she has the maturity to make a wise decision.

A spiritual mother who has been meeting weekly with a young woman should determine when those meetings could become bi-weekly or monthly or even when it is time to stop regular meetings.

None of these illustrations means that we are to cease giving advice or opinions, but they do mean that we are not to use such situations to control. We are to look for opportunities to encourage the younger woman to shift her dependence to God. We should also find ways to acknowledge the younger woman's adulthood and to establish a new balance in the relationship. For the Christian, that new balance is mutual dependence on God.

When our son, Richie, married Shannon, it was an answer to prayer. She is exactly what we had asked the Lord to give Richie. I wanted very much to communicate to them both that I had confidence in Shannon and that I was "releasing" Richie. As I prayed about this, I thought of tangible "stuff" that represented Richie. I thought about his silver baby cup and spoon, the little hospital bracelet he wore at birth, the baby rattle with his birthdate and weight inscribed on it, etc. I had these things framed in a shadowbox and gave them to Shannon. I told her that I was giving her visible representations of Richie's history because I was thrilled that he would spend his future with her. I admit that it was hard to part with those things, but separating with those treasures produced something far richer—a closer relationship with Richie and Shannon.

The Ministry of Spiritual Mothering

Paul's words to the church in Thessalonica are a beautiful summation of the ministry of spiritual mothering:

As apostles of Christ we could have been a burden to you, but we were gentle among you, like a mother caring for her little children. We loved you so much that we were delighted to share with you not only the gospel of God but our lives as well, because you had become so dear to us. (1 Thessalonians 2:6–8)

Paul shared the gospel with them—he equipped them. In the context of sharing his life, a nurturing relationship that encouraged. And he was delighted to do it!

But the relationship with the Thessalonians was not one-sided. This relationship worked because they were teachable:

And we also thank God continually because, when you received the word of God, which you heard from us, you accepted it not as the word of men, but as it actually is, the word of God, which is at work in you who believe. (1 Thessalonians 2:13)

And Paul could celebrate the results:

For what is our hope, our joy, or the crown in which we will glory in the presence of our Lord Jesus when he comes? Is it not you? Indeed, you are our glory and joy. (1 Thessalonians 2:19–20)

Even when he "separated," he continued to be involved in their lives by praying for them:

May the Lord make your love increase and overflow for each other and for everyone else, just as ours does for you. May he strengthen your hearts so that you will be blameless and holy in the presence of our God and Father when our Lord Jesus comes with all his holy ones. Finally, brothers [sisters], we instructed you how to live in order to please God, as in fact you are living. Now we ask you and urge you in the Lord Jesus to do this more and more. (1 Thessalonians 3:12–4:1)

And the relationship continued to give mutual strength, encouragement, and joy to Paul and the Thessalonians.

But Timothy has just now come to us from you and has brought good news about your faith and love. He has told us that you always have pleasant memories of us and that you long to see us, just as we also long to see you. Therefore, brothers [sisters], in all our distress and persecution we were encouraged about you because of your faith. For now we really live, since you are standing firm in the Lord. How can we thank God enough for you in return for all the joy we have in the presence of our God because of you? (1 Thessalonians 3:6–9)

Kay James has an uncompromising witness for Christ in the government arena. When Kay learned that her mother only had a few months to live, Kay decided to leave her position as Director of Public Relations for Right to Life so that she could spend more time with her mother. Then came a call from the Bush administration asking her to accept an appointment as Assistant Secretary for Public Affairs in the Department of Health and Human Services. She declined.

When Kay visited her mother in the hospital, she told her of the call. "And what did you tell them?" her mother asked.

"Why Mom, I told them no. I want to spend more time with you," was her reply.

"You did *what!* Girl, I thought I taught you better than that. How many women—how many *black* women—have an opportunity like that! You call them back and tell them you were just teasing."[2]

Thus Kay James' Christian influence continues to be a factor in Washington. It was more important to a dying mother for her daughter to *serve* the King than to *stay* with her.

Giving birth and nurturing are two of the most profound and noble ways God enables women to glorify Him. Not every woman can give biological birth, but every Christian woman can enter the high calling of spiritual reproduction and motherhood. Our biological clock does not alter this ability. In fact, we actually get better at it after the biological clock winds down!

My dear sister in Christ, don't be relationship-poor and deprive yourself of the privilege of spiritually mothering younger women. Your life has great value. Wherever you are on life's time-line, the experiences you have been through and the faith-lessons you have learned are worth perpetuating. Even as you look back and find a younger woman to nurture, I urge you to look ahead and avail yourself of the perspective of an older woman.

Not every woman can give biological birth, but every Christian woman can enter the high calling of spiritual reproduction and motherhood.

You will be richer—other women will be encouraged and equipped—God will be glorified—His Word will be honored!

I also appeal to you to invest in other women because of the influence women have in shaping our world. In *Women Beyond Equal Rights*, my friend Dee Jepsen quotes the French philosopher Alexis de Tocqueville:

> And now that I come near the end of the book in which I have recorded so many considerable achievements of the Americans, if anyone asks me what I think the chief cause of the extraordinary prosperity and growing power of the nation, I should answer that it is due to the superiority of their women.[3]

Then Dee goes on to say:

> The women of this country ARE special. WOMEN are special. We do bring a quality to life which cannot be duplicated by men. Society needs us and men need us. Women can be the key to our future. . . . If women were to deny their special qualities, their true gifts as women, trying to model themselves after men, all of society would be distorted. Sensitive, loyal, faithful, brave, committed, women willing to be used of God to speak His truth boldly would be sadly absent. . . . In our society today . . . women are center stage. The spotlight of public attention is upon us. The question is, now what are

we going to do with it? I believe, from the ranks of those women who are willing to serve Him, God is assembling a mighty army of women—women who will serve God and their generation, women who will introduce those seeking identity, fulfillment, purpose, and peace to that prince of Peace, the True Liberator: Jesus Christ.[4]

The stories throughout this book are a variegated presentation of women who touched the lives of other women. As I reflect on the stories of these women, I am struck with their willingness to get involved, their willingness to be a part of that "mighty army of women."

Involvement means taking risks, getting tired, and sometimes getting hurt. But I challenge you, my sister, to write your story into the fabric of another woman's life. This is not a call to a life of ease. It is a call to a life of involvement in serving the King by nurturing his daughters. I understand your hesitation, for you see . . .

> I would rather
>> clutch my invitation
>> and wait my turn
>> in party clothes
>> prim, proper
>> safe and clean.
>
> But a pulsing hand
>> keeps driving me
>> over peaks
>> ravines
>> and spidered brambles.
>
> So, I'll pant
>> up to the pearled knocker
>> tattered
>> breathless
>> and full of tales.[5]

We must not waffle. We must write more tales.

Ten months ago my first granddaughter, Mary Kate, was born. My feelings about calling women to spiritual motherhood intensified dramatically when I held that beautiful child in my arms and looked into her face. Women of faith, do not leave Mary Kate with no spiritual mothers. Please tradition Biblical womanhood to her generation.

My prayer is that you have been stimulated to become a spiritual mother. But I also pray that in some way you have been spiritually mothered through reading this book. I pray that in some small way this book has done for you what Elizabeth did for Mary and that you have been encouraged and equipped to live for God's glory. If that has happened, let's join Mary in her song of celebration and praise. And Mary said:

> My soul praises the Lord
>   and my spirit rejoices in God my Savior,
> for he has been mindful
>   of the humble state of his servant.
> From now on all generations
>   will call me blessed,
> for the Mighty One has done great
>   things for me—holy is his name.
> His mercy extends to those who fear him,
>   from generation to generation.
> He has performed mighty deeds with his arm;
>   he has scattered those who are
>   proud in their inmost thoughts.
> He has brought down rulers from their thrones
>   but has lifted up the humble.
> He has filled the hungry with good things
>   but has sent the rich away empty.
> He has helped his servant Israel,
>   remembering to be merciful
> to Abraham and his descendants forever,
> even as he said to our fathers.
>   (Luke 1:46–55)

A Spiritual Mothering Challenge

1. Prayerfully translate the things you have read into action. Perhaps the following questions will help:

   a. What difference has this book made in your thinking? Write out your thoughts.

   b. How are you obeying the Titus mandate? How do you plan to obey it?

   c. Does the women's ministry in your church encourage older-women/younger-women relationships? Could studying this book together promote spiritual mothering?

2. Will you make yourself available to God to be used to nurture another woman?

NOTES

Introduction

1. The Leader's Guide for this book gives a lesson plan for the leader, group exercises designed to help groups learn to implement the ideas in the book, and worksheets to be duplicated for participants. To order call the Presbyterian Church in America Bookstore: 1-800-283-1357. Also, *Leadership For Women In the Church*, (Zondervan) co-authored with my friend Peggy Hutcheson, and the companion Leader's Guide, give information and group exercises to help a group explore the related issue of using the full range of women's gifts in the local church.

Chapter 1: Our Reference Point

1. Mary Foxwell Loeks, *The Glorious Names of God* (Grand Rapids, MI: Baker, 1986), 107–108.

2. John Calvin, *Calvin's Commentaries, Isaiah, Vol. IV* (Grand Rapids, MI: Eerdmans, 1956), 30–31.

3. John MacArthur's Bible Studies, *Exposing False Spiritual Leaders* Matthew 23, (Panorama, City, CA: Word of Grace Communications, 1986), 113.

4. Dee Jepsen, *Women Beyond Equal Rights* (Waco, TX: Word, 1984), 227, cited in Ibid.

Chapter 3: The Command

1. William Hendriksen, *New Testament Commentary, I-II Timothy and Titus* (Grand Rapids, MI: Baker, 1957), 362–363.

2. Dee Jepsen, *Women Beyond Equal Rights* (Waco: Word, 1984), quoted in James Robinson, *Attack on the Family* (Wheaton, IL: Tyndale House Publishers, 1981), 33.

3. W. E. Vine, *An Expository Dictionary of New Testament Words* Vol. IV (Old Tappan, NJ: Revell), 44.

4. Cecil Williamson, *The Eunice Fellowship: A Manual To Help Involve Older Women in Ministries to Younger Women in the Local Congregation*, in partial fulfillment for the Doctor of Ministry degree of Westminster Theological Seminary, Philadelphia, 9.

Chapter 4: The Curriculum

1. Francis Schaeffer, *The Church at the End of the 20th Century* (Downer's Grove, IL: Intervarsity Press, 1990), 137.

2. James Dobson'S *Tough Love* and James Alsdurf and Phyllis Alsdurf's *Battered Into Submission* are helpful in this area.

3. Amy Saltzman, "Troulbe at the Top," *U.S. News and World Report*, June, 1991.

4. Elisabeth Elliot, *A Chance to Die: The Life of Amy Carmichael* (Old Tappan, NJ: Fleming H. Revell Co., 1987), 15.

Chapter 6: Encourage and Equip

1. *New American Standard Exhaustive Concordance of the Bible* (Nashville, TN: Holman, 1981), 1,653.

2. "On Speaking Terms With Friends," by Joseph F. Ryan, in *Tabletalk*, April 1991, Ligonier Ministries.

Chapter 8: The Ministry of Encouragement

Author's note: Larry Crabb, *Encouragement: The Key To Caring* is recommended for a deeper look at this subject.

1. Jay E. Adams, *The Big Umbrella* (Nutley, TN: Presbyterian and Reformed Publishing Company, 1972), 251.

2. Ibid.

3. Ibid, 252.

Chapter 9: The Power of Acceptance

1. Marshall Shelley, *Well-Intentioned Dragons* (Co-published by Christianity Today, Inc., and Word, Inc., 1985), 11.

2. *The Atlanta Journal/Constitution*, Saturday, July 6, 1991.

3. James C. Dobson, *Straight Talk to Men and Their Wives* (Waco, TX: Word, 1984), 109.

Chapter 10: The Cornerstone of Acceptance

Author's note: The topic of forgiveness cannot possibly be covered in one chapter. Recommended reading on this topic include: *Disappointment with God*, by Philip Yancey and *The Freedom of Forgiveness*, by David Augsburger.

1. Arthur W. Pink, *The Life of David* (Grand Rapids, MI: Baker, 1981), 134.

2. Dr. Larry Crabb, *Men & Women: Enjoying the Difference* (Grand Rapids, MI: Zondervan, 1991), 13.

3. Corrie ten Boom with John and Elizabeth Sherrill, *The Hiding Place* (Old Tappan, NJ: World Wide Publications by Spire Books, 1971), 217.

4. Ibid., 236.

5. Ibid., 238.

6. Elisabeth Elliot, *The Savage My Kinsman* (Ann Arbor, MI: Servant Books, 1961), 6.

7. Gail MacDonald, *Keep Climbing* (Wheaton, IL: Tyndale House Publishers, Inc., 1989), 79.

Chapter 11: Comfort the Comfortless

1. Elisabeth Elliot, *A Chance to Die*, 52.

2. Ibid., cited from Mildred Cable and Francesca French, *A Woman Who Laughed: Biography of Henrietta Soltau*, 59, 154ff.

Chapter 12: Staying . . . and Separating

1. Shannon Brownlee, *U.S. News and World Report*, "Conversation: Daughters' Lives," September 24, 1990.

2. From Kay James' address to the Presbyterian Church in America's 1989 National Women In the Church conference.

3. Quoted from Alexis de Tocqueville, *Democracy in America*, trans. George Lawrence,1835, reprint (Garden City, N.Y.: Doubleday, Anchor Books, 1969), 603; cited by Jepsen, 220.

4. Ibid., 220, 229, 230.

5. Janet Chester Bly, *Managing Your Restless Search* (Wheaton, IL: Victor Books, SP Publications, 1992), 10.

$\mathcal{A}$BOUT THE AUTHOR

S usan Hunt is a pastor's wife. She and her husband, Gene, have three adult children and eleven grandchildren. She currently serves as the Women's Ministry Consultant for the Presbyterian Church in America's Christian Education and Publications. She has degrees from the University of South Carolina and Columbia Theological Seminary.

Susan may be contacted at PCA Christian Education and Publications, 1700 N. Brown Rd., Lawrenceville, GA 30043, phone 678-825-1100.

Parts of the Whole

Just as we are each part of the whole family of Christ worldwide and throughout generations, so these books support and complement one another. Throughout each runs a theme of living covenantally—of seeing the wide expanse of God's mercy and grace to us intricately woven into every relationship and detail of life—and passing the legacy on to others.

LEAVING A LEGACY

Heirs of the Covenant—While today's broken culture grasps for direction, you can discover what happens when the church offers true Christian education and you fulfill your calling to leave a legacy of faith for the next generation.

TPB, ISBN 1-58134-011-7, $13.99

FASHION A LIFE WHERE GOD IS WELCOME

Your Home: A Place of Grace—Explore how covenant values help you fashion a life where God is welcome, a heart where He freely lives and a spiritual home that realizes the joy of His presence every day.

TPB, ISBN 1-58134-185-7, $12.99

FOR YOU AS A WOMAN

By Design—A joyous celebration of God's "helper" design for women that will challenge you to explore the significance of your biblical calling and rally the church to equip one of its greatest resources: you.

TPB, ISBN 0-89107-976-9, $12.99

THE BEAUTY AND STRENGTH OF GODLY WOMEN

The True Woman—Set your heart on fire and get excited about the unique opportunity you have as a godly woman to make a difference for eternity as you discover how to reflect Christ in all areas of life.

TPB, ISBN 0-89107-927-0, $12.99

TELLING THE NEXT GENERATION

Big Truths—Teach your kids the basics of the Christian faith with this fun, illustrated book. Its stories of everyday situations will help them integrate those truths in a way that finds expression at home, at school, and with friends. Ages 3 to 8.

HC, ISBN 1-58134-106-7, $15.99

A FUN WAY TO LEARN BIBLICAL VALUE

My ABC Bible Verses—A colorful, story-filled way for even your youngest child to take God's Word to heart—and learn the alphabet too! It's a great resource for teaching biblical values to your kids at home, school, or church. Ages 3-7.

HC, ISBN 1-58134-005-2, $14.99